IARIA



# INTELLI 2025

The Fourteenth International Conference on Intelligent Systems and Applications

March 9th –13th, 2025

Lisbon, Portugal

**INTELLI 2025 Editors**

Gil Gonçalves, University of Porto, Portugal

**Printed from e-media with permission by:**

Curran Associates, Inc.
57 Morehouse Lane
Red Hook, NY 12571

**Some format issues inherent in the e-media version may also appear in this print version.**



International Academy, Research, and Industry Association (IARIA)
412 Derby Way
Wilmington, DE 19810

Phone: (408) 893-6407
Fax: (408) 527-6351

petre@iaria.org

**Additional copies of this publication are available from:**

Curran Associates, Inc.
57 Morehouse Lane
Red Hook, NY 12571 USA
Phone: 845-758-0400
Fax: 845-758-2633
Email: curran@proceedings.com
Web: www.proceedings.com

**Table of Contents**

Fursight: A Fully Integrated Solution for Pet Monitoring via CPS and IoT 1
*Antonio Santos, Joao Araujo, Jorge Sousa, Jose Castro, Guilherme Sequeira, Miguel Montes, Pedro Ramalho, Ricardo Inacio, Vitor Cavaleiro, Rui Pinto, and Gil Goncalves*

Automation of Beer Dispensers: A Cyber-Physical System Solution 8
*Lorenzo Piarulli, Luca Di Pietro, Jose A. Gaspar, Miguel A. Teixeira, Jaume Sansano, Lucas Sousa, Luis Paiva, Emanuel Gestosa, Alexandre Correia, Rui Pinto, and Gil Goncalves*

SmartPool: An Automated CPS-Based System for Real-Time Water Quality Management 15
*Andre Avila, Andre C. Costa, Andre Soares, Daniel Rodrigues, Eduardo T. Ramos, Joao Alves, Joao C. Matos, Lourenco Goncalves, Luis Cabral, Marco Rocha, Rui Pinto, and Gil Goncalves*

Situated Independent Learners in a Sequential Decision-Making Setting 21
*Timur Kasimov, Shinon Takei, Hanfeng Lu, Mingi Lee, and Fernanda Eliott*

Vessel Route Planning Optimization Combined with Time Windows versus Work Scheduling for Offshore Windmill Maintenance 30
*Erik De Kuyffer, Toon De Pessemier, Wout Joseph, and Luc Martens*

Achievement of Collision Avoidance and Formation for Nonlinear Multi-Ship Systems Using an Interval Type-2 Fuzzy Tracking Approach 39
*Wen-Jer Chang and Yann-Horng Lin*

Exploring the Role of User Experience in Enhancing IoT Applications for Smart Manufacturing: A Review 45
*Leigh Johnston, Kyle Madden, Justin Quinn, Sonya Coleman, and Dermot Kerr*

TrustLab: An Interactive Tool for Evaluating Online Trustworthiness across Diverse Domains 51
*Teng-Chieh Huang, Wenting Song, Brian Kim, and Suzanne Barber*

# INTELLI 2025

# Forward

The Fourteenth International Conference on Intelligent Systems and Applications (INTELLI 2025), held between March 9th, 2025, and March 13th, 2025, in Lisbon, Portugal, continued a series of international events on advances towards fundamental, as well as practical and experimental, aspects of intelligent systems and applications.

The information surrounding us is not only overwhelming but also subject to limitations of systems and applications, including specialized devices. The diversity of systems and the spectrum of situations make it almost impossible for an end-user to handle the complexity of the challenges. Embedding intelligence in systems and applications seems to be a reasonable way to move some complex tasks away from the user. However, this approach requires fundamental changes in designing the systems and applications, in designing their interfaces, and requires using specific cognitive and collaborative mechanisms. Intelligence has become a key paradigm, and its specific use takes various forms according to the technology or the domain a system or an application belongs to.

We take here the opportunity to warmly thank all the members of the INTELLI 2025 technical program committee, as well as all the reviewers. The creation of such a high-quality conference program would not have been possible without their involvement. We also kindly thank all the authors who dedicated much of their time and effort to contribute to INTELLI 2025. We truly believe that, thanks to all these efforts, the final conference program consisted of top-quality contributions. We also thank the members of the INTELLI 2025 organizing committee for their help in handling the logistics of this event.

We hope that INTELLI 2025 was a successful international forum for the exchange of ideas and results between academia and industry for the promotion of progress in the field of intelligent systems and applications.

**INTELLI 2025 Chairs**

**INTELLI 2025 Steering Committee**
Carsten Behn, Schmalkalden University of Applied Sciences, Germany
Stefano Berretti, University of Firenze, Italy
Marcin Paprzycki, Systems Research Institute, Polish Academy of Sciences – Warszawa, Poland
Gil Gonçalves, University of Porto, Portugal

**INTELLI 2025 Publicity Chairs**
Francisco Javier Díaz Blasco, Universitat Politècnica de València, Spain
Ali Ahmad, Universitat Politècnica de València, Spain
José Miguel Jiménez, Universitat Politècnica de València, Spain
Sandra Viciano Tudela, Universitat Politècnica de València, Spain

## INTELLI 2025
## Committee

### INTELLI 2025 Steering Committee

Carsten Behn, Schmalkalden University of Applied Sciences, Germany
Stefano Berretti, University of Firenze, Italy
Marcin Paprzycki, Systems Research Institute, Polish Academy of Sciences – Warszawa, Poland
Gil Gonçalves, University of Porto, Portugal

### INTELLI 2025 Publicity Chairs

Francisco Javier Díaz Blasco, Universitat Politècnica de València, Spain
Ali Ahmad, Universitat Politècnica de València, Spain
José Miguel Jiménez, Universitat Politècnica de València, Spain
Sandra Viciano Tudela, Universitat Politècnica de València, Spain

### INTELLI 2025 Technical Program Committee

Azizi Ab Aziz, Universiti Utara Malaysia, Malaysia
Lounis Adouane, Université de Technologie de Compiègne, France
Leo Aguilera, 33 Technologies LLC, USA
Ari Aharari, SOJO University, Japan
Bilal Ahmad, University of Warwick, UK
Sathish Akula, Florida Polytechnic University, USA
Zaher Al Aghbari, University of Sharjah, UAE
Miltos Alamaniotis, University of Texas at San Antonio, USA
Antonios Alexos, University of California Irvine, USA
Sarra Alqahtani, Wake Forest University, USA
Rachid Anane, Coventry University, UK
Olugbenga Moses Anubi, Florida State University, USA
Arvind Bansal, Kent State University, USA
Suzanne Barber, The University of Texas at Austin, USA
Dariusz Barbucha, Gdynia Maritime University, Poland
Carmelo Bastos-Filho, University of Pernambuco, Brazil
Rafael Batres, Tecnologico de Monterrey, Mexico
Carsten Behn, Schmalkalden University of Applied Sciences, Germany
Fayçal Bensaali, Qatar University, Qatar
Lyes Benyoucef, Aix-Marseille University, France
Giuseppe Berio, IRISA | Université de Bretagne Sud, France
Stefano Berretti, University of Firenze, Italy
Jonathan Berrisch, University of Duisburg-Essen, Germany
Mahdis Bisheban, National Research Council Canada (NRC), Canada
José Miguel Blanco, Masaryk University, Brno, Czech Republic
Francisco Bonin Font, University of the Balearic Islands, Spain
Lucas Botoni de Souza, Federal University of Technology - Paraná, Brazil
Frederic Bousefsaf, LCOMS | Université de Lorraine, France

Simeon C. Calvert, Delft University of Technology, Netherlands
Valérie Camps, Paul Sabatier University | IRIT, Toulouse, France
Carlos Carrascosa, Universitat Politècnica de València, Spain
Cesar Castelo-Fernandez, Institute of Computing | University of Campinas, Brazil
Martin Cech, University of West Bohemia, Pilsen, Czech Republic
Coskun Cetinkaya, Kennesaw State University, USA
Chin-Chen Chang, Feng Chia University, Taiwan
Tongwen Chen, University of Alberta, Canada
Guilherme Conde, Federal University of Western Pará, Brazil
Angelo Croatti, University of Bologna, Italy
Daniela D'Auria, Free University of Bozen-Bolzano, Italy
Mohammed Dahane, Université de Lorraine, France
Robertas Damaševičius, Silesian University of Technology, Poland
Chuangyin Dang, City University of Hong Kong, Hong Kong
Andrea D'Ariano, Roma Tre University, Italy
Jos De Brabanter, KU Leuven ESAT-STADIUS, Belgium
Toon De Pessemier, imec - WAVES - Ghent University, Belgium
Angel P. del Pobil, Jaume I University, Spain
Dapeng Dong, Xi'an Jiaotong-Liverpool University, China
Jens Dörpinghaus, Federal Institute for Vocational Education and Training (BIBB) / German Center for Neurodegenerative Diseases (DZNE), Germany
Paweł Drąg, Wrocław University of Science and Technology, Poland
Nelson Duarte, CIICESI | ESTG | Politécnico do Porto, Portugal / IRIEM, Hong Kong
Arianna D'Ulizia, National Research Council - IRPPS, Italy
Nourhan Ehab, German University in Cairo, Egypt
Khaoula ElBedoui, LIMTIC | ENICarthage - University of Carthage, Tunisia
Tullio Facchinetti, University of Pavia, Italy
Ana Fernández Vilas, School of Telecommunication Engineering | University of Vigo, Spain
Stefka Fidanova, IICT-BAS, Sofia, Bulgaria
Manuel Filipe Santos, University of Minho, Portugal
Edgar Giovanny Cuzco Silva, Universidad Nacional de Chimborazo, Ecuador
Todorka Glushkova, Plovdiv University "Paisii Hilendarski", Bulgaria
Helder Gomes Costa, Universidade Federal Fluminese (UFF), Brazil
Gil Gonçalves, University of Porto, Portugal
Sérgio Gorender, Federal University of Bahia, Brazil
Javier Gozalvez, Universidad Miguel Hernandez de Elche, Spain
Emmanuelle Grislin-Le Strugeon, LAMIH | Université Polytechnique Hauts-de-France (UPHF), France
Yousif A. Hamad, Imam Ja'afar Al-Sadiq University, Iraq / Siberian Federal University, Russia
Ibrahim A. Hameed, Norwegian University of Science and Technology (NTNU), Norway
Wahida Handouzi, Tlemcen University, Algeria
Wladyslaw Homenda, Warsaw University of Technology, Poland
Tzung-Pei Hong, National University of Kaohsiung, Taiwan
Wei-Chiang Hong, School of Education Intelligent Technology - Jiangsu Normal University, China
Kuo-Chan Huang, National Taichung University of Education, Taiwan
Chih-Cheng Hung, Kennesaw State University - Marietta Campus, USA
Syed Muhammad Zeeshan Iqbal, BrightWare LLC, Riyadh, Saudi Arabia
Zahid Iqbal, University of Porto, Portugal
Ajune Wanis Ismail, Universiti Teknologi Malaysia, Malaysia

Debajyoti Mukhopadhyay, Mumbai University, India
Muddasar Naeem, ICAR-CNR, Naples, Italy
Filippo Neri, University of Naples, Italy
Pranav Ajeet Nerurkar, NMIMS University, Mumbai, India
Dinh-Luan Nguyen, Michigan State University, USA
Thanh-Tuan Nguyen, HCMC University of Technology and Education, HCM City, Vietnam / University of Toulon, CNRS, LIS, Toulon, France
Alex Norta, Tallinn University of Technology, Estonia
Cyrus F. Nourani, akdmkrd.tripod.com, USA
Kenneth Nwizege, Ken Saro-Wiwa Polytechnic, Nigeria
Jin Dong, Oak Ridge National Laboratory, USA
Michel Occello, Université Grenoble Alpes, France
Krzysztof Okarma, West Pomeranian University of Technology in Szczecin, Poland
Ana Oliveira Alves, Coimbra Polytechnic - ISEC & Centre of Informatics and Systems of the University of Coimbra - CISUC, Portugal
Joanna Isabelle Olszewska, University of West Scotland, UK
Yash-Vardhan Pant, University of California, Berkeley, USA
Marcin Paprzycki, Systems Research Institute / Polish Academy of Sciences - Warsaw, Poland
Carla Pereira, School of Technology and Management / INESC TEC, Portugal
Isidoros Perikos, University of Patras, Greece
Goharik Petrosyan, International Scientific-Educational Center of the National Academy of Sciences, Yerevan, Armenia
Agostino Poggi, Università degli Studi di Parma, Italy
Marco Polignano, University of Bari "Aldo Moro", Italy
Filipe Portela, University of Minho, Portugal
Catia Prandi, University of Bologna, Italy
Dilip Kumar Pratihar, Indian Institute of Technology Kharagpur, India
Radu-Emil Precup, Politehnica University of Timisoara, Romania
Shahnawaz Qureshi, National University of Computer and Emerging Sciences, Pakistan
Ahmed Rafea, American University in Cairo, Egypt
Giuliana Ramella, National Research Council (CNR) - Institute for the Applications of Calculus "M. Picone" (IAC), Italy
Chakroun Rania, National School of Engineering of Sfax | Advanced Technologies for Image and Signal Processing (ATISP) Research Unit, Sfax, Tunisia
Radha Reddy, CISTER Research Center | ISEP | FEUP, Porto, Portugal
Carlos Renato Vázquez, Tecnológico de Monterrey, Mexico
Fátima Rodrigues, Institute of Engineering |¬ Polytechnic of Porto, Portugal
Daniel Rodriguez, University of Alcalá, Spain
Federica Rollo, University of Modena and Reggio Emilia, Italy
Peter Rössler, University of Applied Sciences Technikum Wien, Austria
Amirreza Rouhi, Politecnico di Milano, Italy
Alexander Ryjov, Lomonosov Moscow State University | Russian Presidential Academy of National Economy and Public Administration, Russia
Fariba Sadri, Imperial College London, UK
Mohammad Saeid Mahdavinejad, Kansas State University, USA
Bilal Abu Salih, Curtin University, Australia
Demetrios Sampson, Curtin University, Australia
Christophe Sauvey, LGIPM | Université de Lorraine, France

Alessandra Scotto di Freca, Università di Cassino e del Lazio Meridionale, Italy
Chantal Soulé-Dupuy, University of Toulouse Capitole, France
Sashank Sridhar, College of Engineering Guindy - Anna University, India
Mark Terwilliger, University of North Alabama, USA
Supphachai Thaicharoen, Srinakharinwirot University, Bangkok, Thailand
Pei-Wei Tsai, Swinburne University of Technology, Australia
Berna Ulutas, Eskisehir Osmangazi University, Turkey
Paulo Urbano, Universidade de Lisboa - BioISI, Portugal
Jan Vascak, Technical University of Kosice, Slovakia
Costas Vassilakis, University of the Peloponnese, Greece
Anna-Maria Velentza, University of Macedonia, Thessaloniki, Greece
Minjuan Wang, San Diego State University, USA
Yifei Wang, Georgia Institute of Technology, USA
Kanoksak Wattanachote, Guangdong University of Foreign Study, China
Dietmar Winkler, TU Wien | CDL-SQI, Vienna, Austria
Stefanie Wuschitz, Miss Baltazar's Laboratory, Vienna, Austria
Mudasser F. Wyne, National University, USA
Maria Gabriella Xibilia, University of Messina, Italy
Wenju Xu, Amazon, USA
Longzhi Yang, Northumbria University, UK
Leila Zemmouchi-Ghomari, Ecole Nationale Supérieure de Technologie, ENST, Algiers, Algeria

## Copyright Information

# Fursight: A Fully Integrated Solution for Pet Monitoring via CPS and IoT

António Santos[†, 1], João Araújo[†, 1], Jorge Sousa[†, 1], José Castro[†, 1], Guilherme Sequeira[†, 1], Miguel Montes[†, 1], Pedro Ramalho[†, 1], Ricardo Inácio[†, 1], Vítor Cavaleiro[†, 1], Rui Pinto[1,2], Gil Gonçalves[1,2]

Dept. of Informatics Engineering, Faculty of Engineering, University of Porto, Porto, Portugal[1]
SYSTEC, ARISE, Faculty of Engineering, University of Porto, Porto, Portugal[2]
Email: {up202008004, up202004293, up202006140, up202006963, up202004648, up202007516, up202004715, up202302742, up202004724}@up.pt
{rpinto, gil}@fe.up.pt
[†]These authors contributed equally to this work.

***Abstract*—The paper proposes a novel, fully integrated intelligent system that incorporates the Internet of Things and Cyber-Physical Systems technologies to streamline the routine of monitoring household pets' day-to-day life and well-being. By leveraging this system, users become keenly aware of the overall disposition of their pets, allowing for a multimodal data-driven approach to responsible care. Several data collection devices are leveraged to collect information about the current circumstances of a pet, resulting in derivable, up-to-date insights available to the user on the web. Several use cases were used to validate this approach, exemplifying the usefulness of a modular pet-care system that is customisable to varying needs and can be seamlessly deployed locally or to the cloud, ensuring well-being at all times. By leveraging current animal monitoring efforts with new-age data collection technologies, Fursight represents a robust solution to unobtrusive pet care, combining the Internet of Things and human-centred design, to reach optimal care even in the prevailing fast-paced mode of life.**

***Keywords-IoT; CPS; pet monitoring; self-deployed applications.***

## I. Introduction

Taking proper care of a pet is a great responsibility. Several factors need to be accounted for at all times regarding the health and well-being of the animal, which could be divided across diverse contexts that must be harmoniously reconciled. The evolving dynamics of human-companion animal relationships are influenced by modern societal trends, including increased emotional attachment, changing family structures, and external factors such as remote work adoption and the COVID-19 pandemic. Research suggests that while some pet owners experience time constraints due to demanding work schedules, others have adjusted their lifestyles to accommodate more interaction with their pets [1].

Wearable technology has emerged as a key enabler in pet monitoring solutions, providing insights into location tracking, health metrics, and behavioural patterns. These devices, such as GPS collars, heart rate monitors, and activity trackers, are widely used for monitoring pets' well-being and have been increasingly integrated with IoT and smart home systems [2]. However, as demonstrated with *Elizabethan collars* [3], artefacts placed around the throat contribute to distress and discomfort. Adversely, the ever-growing array of options for circumstance monitoring in data collection devices commonly used in Internet of Things (IoT) solutions (e.g., smart room sensors) lay the groundwork for a non-invasive and easily implementable option towards animal companion care. With all of this, an application that takes advantage of the availability of connected systems would be extremely valuable, allowing for continuous and accessible monitoring even when pets need to be left unattended.

Recent advancements in Cyber-Physical Systems (CPS) have facilitated their integration into smart home environments, enhancing automation, security, and remote monitoring capabilities. These developments have led to the widespread adoption of intelligent systems for pet care, enabling real-time monitoring, interactive communication, and adaptive behavioural analysis [4].

In this context, the authors propose a solution, designated Fursight [5]. This solution conducts all its sensing at the Edge, leaving analysis and processing to the central hub, leveraging wireless connectivity to transmit the collected data. By aggregating environment data, valuable insights can be provided to further enhance several care processes. In this sense, different *Arduino Nano* flavours, linked to diverse sensors and actuators, connect to a *Raspberry Pi Model 4* [6] to build a cohesive system which effectively exchanges data across all components. Through `Node-RED` [7], workflows for automatic data processing can be defined, allowing for seamless deployment of different settings by simply swapping configuration files. Hence, such a system can be deployed in any home division where pets may be settled, either locally or online, to streamline the care processes based on insights derived from data. Information is then stored securely, and made available through a web interface that displays to the user visualisations of the sensed environment. Through the installation of an integrated container [8], all the necessary resources are automatically loaded, easily enabling full functionality.

This paper is organized as follows: this Introduction Section I, which outlines the challenges, motivations, and objectives of this work, is followed by the Related Work Section II, which highlights fundamental in-domain research, including a critical analysis of existing solutions to underscore the necessity of this approach. The Proposed Solution Section III elaborates on the proposition, detailing the solution architecture and implementation process, along with the technologies employed. In the Evaluation Section IV, the results of the carried-out tests are presented, incorporating assessment methodologies, and a thorough analysis of the outcomes. The Discussion Section V provides a breakdown of the findings, emphasizing the benefits of the solution while addressing its limitations and identifying areas for potential enhancement. The paper concludes with a Conclusion and Future Work Section VI, which highlights the key contributions and achievements of the study and outlines directions for prospective endeavours.

## II. Related Work

In this section, the background that serves as the foundation of the proposed solution is presented. Firstly, related technologies and similar solutions in the current literature are analysed, subsequently showcasing the current gaps addressed in the proposed solution. Presently, most solutions are based on the same set of core technologies, as they are long-standing standards in the field of home automation and connectivity.

The advancements in communication technologies, alongside the decrease in complexity of home automation and monitoring systems, allow for specific solutions that exploit the continuous availability these techniques provide. Thus, several works have been developed recently, to harness these advantages in the context of pet monitoring and care. These are divided across several modalities, such as: wearables that continuously monitor vitals and geolocation; cameras that constantly provide image or video feeds; automatic feeders and water dispensers based on actuators; software apps and platforms, that provide relevant information and aggregate data to deliver insights. For a more holistic assessment of such approaches, refer to the survey about pet care technology [9].

### A. Wearables for Continuous Monitoring

Most health and vitals monitoring solutions for pets rely on wearable devices, typically attached via a collar or specialized accessories. For example, Reyu and Princess [10] propose a wearable system that tracks heart rate, temperature, activity levels, and location. However, research suggests that such devices may cause discomfort if they are too obtrusive [3].

In addition to the wearable, their system includes a monitoring application designed to aggregate and display collected data. While no specific mobile architecture is specified, they plan to provide a web-based platform to ensure broader compatibility across devices. Their approach also incorporates machine learning techniques to analyze trends and predict potential health issues, enhancing proactive pet care.

### B. Multimedia Capturing Technologies

In the vision modality, the use of image and video capturing technology provides owners with an opportunity to continuously supervise their pets, from any place from which connectivity is available. However, a continuous acquisition of such data results in vast amounts of storage space occupied. Furthermore, only a portion of the recorded events are relevant to the owners, as the majority will consist of mundane activities. This issue is further amplified by the limited resources commonly inherent to IoT devices, which also indirectly pose security risks, as secure and complex encryption may not be feasible, relying on simpler methods instead [11]. Thus, given the nature of the service, if the home-based video or image data must be sent to the internet, a secure connection must be ensured.

### C. Automatic Feeders and Water Dispensers

The task of automating the feeding of pets, ensuring they are well-nourished while taking into consideration their specific needs, has been a long-standing effort. It allows owners to ensure the welfare of their pets, even under time or mobility constraints. Advancements in communication technologies, even enable an intelligent feeding process, where food ration sizes are tailored to the pet, based on physical factors and energy requirements [12]. This approach employs a mobile application, paired with a social media account, to remotely control the feeder, schedule feedings, or review feeding history. The benefits can also stem from the possibility of proactive nourishment, given environmental data. For example, if the temperature increases, the water delivery rate could increase as well [13]. However, this association with mobile applications, inadvertently reduces the scope of the install base of the service, as a forced addition of social features may lead to technological anxiety [14], showcasing the need for advanced and digitally integrated, but local, private solutions.

### D. Software-based Solutions

Lastly, software-based apps and platforms, developed to either complement the previously mentioned solutions or as standalone services, to aid in pet monitoring and care, are wide-ranging. Some examples that follow the previous procedures are companion apps for live feed cameras and automatic feeders. Some integrate popular AI assistant technology, such as *Google Assistant* [15], to streamline some tasks. Standalone apps that do not require external tools can be valuable, as they reap the benefits brought by mobile computing. They allow users to log veterinary appointments, medications, and vaccinations, or to set reminders for boosters. Other apps allow activity and behaviour tracking, to enhance the level of detail and quality of the care provided. Social features allow for exchanging relevant knowledge, such as training and grooming tips, promoting pet well-being [16], although such focus on applications can lead to negative perception [14], as already mentioned.

## III. Proposed Solution

In this section, the methodology behind the proposed approach is presented, alongside the development and implementation details undertaken to reach the final solution. It tries to solve several problems using a package that encompasses features related to the modalities presented in the Related Work Section II. Figure 1 details the overarching design and architecture of the implemented solution, where two Arduino

(X and Y), connected to two submodels each (sensor and actuator), send gathered raw data to the local central hub via the Internet protocol suite (TCP/IP) [17]. An advanced submodule, specifically a serial camera, can be connected to the hub. Using `RabbitMQ` [18], this hub can either send the processed, gathered data to a local, self-hosted server, or to the cloud, to as many servers as it needs, given specific requirements. The engineered architecture was tailored to provide every functionality coherently while also allowing for a distributed approach toward reliance and scalability. It is arranged across three key domains: Physical, Middleware and Application.

### A. Physical Layer

The Physical layer is present at a local level in each client setup. It contains several submodules serving different monitoring and actuating purposes, connected to a central hub for processing and communication. While the central hub works as a hotspot using the Dynamic Host Configuration Protocol (DHCP) in the local network, it is also able to connect securely to servers via TCP/IP [17]. The submodules are comprised of sensors and actuators connected to an *Arduino*, using serial protocols, such as the Inter-Integrated Circuit (I2C) [19], SenseWire (I3C) [20], Serial Peripheral Interface (SPI) [21], and Universal Asynchronous Receiver-Transmitter (UART) [22] protocols for linkage. These, in turn, act as the physical hub for the setup placed on each desired division. Multiple of these, spanning different modalities, can be connected to the central hub to provide a more sophisticated monitoring scheme, enabling multiplicity, as each physical device can be easily tracked and referred to using the identification system. The data collected by the sensors is processed in the *Arduino Nano* modules, which are then sent, via TCP/IP [17] over Wi-Fi, to the local *Raspberry Pi 4 Model B* [6] central hub, using the Message Queue Telemetry Transport (MQTT) [23] broker, implemented via `RabbitMQ` [18]. Additionally, more advanced sensors, such as serial cameras, can be installed directly into the main hub, also interfaced via SPI [21], and streaming in real-time via the User Datagram Protocol (UDP) [24]. If this data must be sent online, a secure connection must be ensured, given the sensitivity of the matter (such as household data). Some practical examples consist of movement and proximity detectors, litter box usage tracking, smart feeding, and audiovisual active monitoring. With this modular setup, the flexibility of the solution allows it to be implemented in almost every possible home environment.

### B. Middleware Layer

The Middleware servers as the centralized processing unit of all the sensed raw local environment data. Thus, it serves as the central hub of the services, which aggregates all the employed physical hubs (i.e., separate physical hubs each in a different room of the house). The scripting capabilities of the `Python` language are employed, given its relevance for data science, and strong support of related libraries [25]. To exchange information with all the locally present submodules, `RabbitMQ` was chosen for the message broker [18]. This technology provides a robust topic-based messaging system, originally implementing the Advanced Message Queuing Protocol (AMQP) [26], later supporting more standard protocols such as MQTT [23]. Each active sensor is assigned an identifier, which then is used as part of the message topic sent through the network. By using message topics with `RabbitMQ` [18], it is ensured that data from specific sources reaches only desired ends while also identifying the modules it went through. Each *Arduino* also has an identifier assigned, which it adds to the message topic, that already contains the identifiers from the sensors. Here, the central hub acts as the core for data processing, so that it can be stored, to then be analysed and converted into valuable knowledge regarding the pet.

For a more private and local approach, the user is able to use their machine to act as a self-hosted server. In this case, the communication is still made through an MQTT [23] broker, ensuring a fast and lightweight transmission, although not very secure, which is not problematic given the isolated facet of the exchange. Before storage, a local implementation of this layer would have a central hub (*Raspberry Pi Model 4* [6]), adding its identifier to the message topic, already containing the ones from each physical hub module the message passed through. However, if the user prefers an always-available solution, then the server can be deployed online with ease, ensuring secure communication via transport protocols like Secure Sockets Layer (SSL) and Transport Layer Security (TCL). This way, it is possible to distribute the load through several servers, or even to keep replicas of important data. In this case, another identifier is added to the complete chain of identifiers, specifying which local client the message is coming from. This process is shown, in a simplified manner, in Figure 1. If this second route is taken, then contents sent to the cloud are pipelined through `Node-RED` [7] in order to streamline data handling. This tool abstracts this process to a higher level, making it useful in systems where inputs may come from diverse sources. It not only allows data to be accessed in real-time but also easy implementation of custom logic for transforming raw sensor data into structured outputs. It is instantiated in the central hub, and not only receives input through MQTT [23] from sensors and servers but also performs specified transformations that support future analyses, such as moving averages for time series. Furthermore, different pipelines can be employed by simply switching the deployed to a JavaScript Object Notation (JSON) configuration.

Ultimately, this layer becomes optional for small-scale, low-cost processing contexts in which there is, for example, only a single-tracked environment. In this case, data can be sent directly to the application layer from the physical hub.

### C. Application Layer

Finally, the Application layer comprises both the backend and frontend of the proposed approach, providing the logic and presentation using the processed data. In the backend, *Supabase* [27] was employed in a Backend as a Service (BaaS)

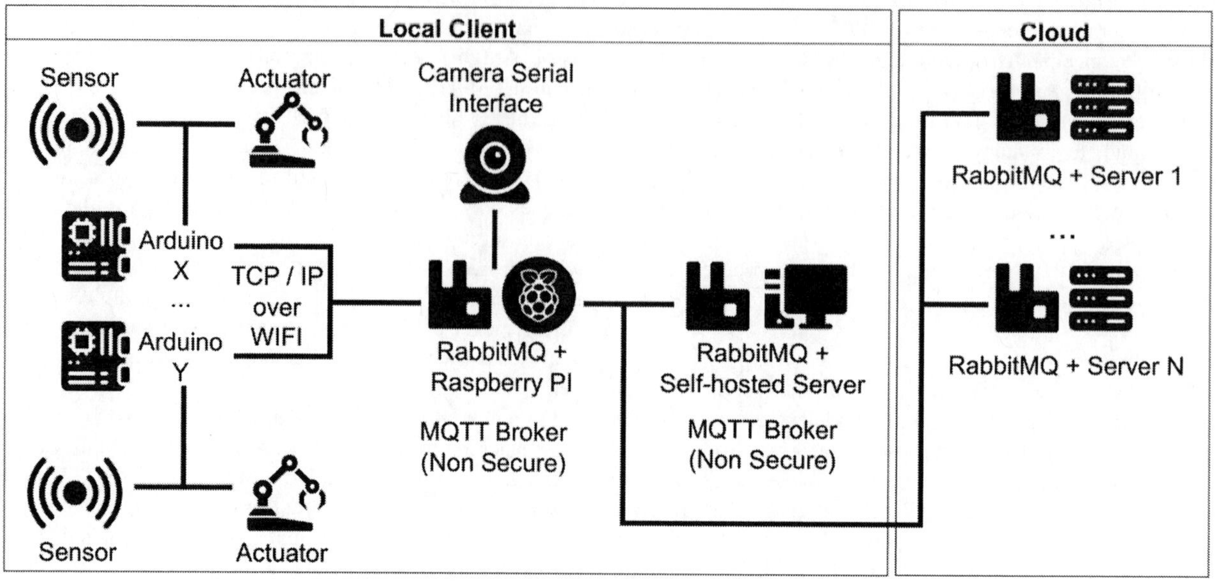


Figure 1. Architecture of the solution.

paradigm, as an authentication-enabled database, to store user-specific location and specification data. Communication at this layer is still made using the previously established `RabbitMQ` settings. Through *Supabase* [27], information related to each user, about the location of service deployment, hardware specifications, and sensor configuration, is saved on different relational tables. To make this data seamlessly accessible, a RESTful API [28] was developed, allowing for CRUD operations on said data (create, read, update, delete). It is then used both on internal Python scripts and via the JavaScript *fetch* API to display extracted knowledge and insights to the end user. Regarding authentication, several options are available so that end users may choose their preferred method. If it is the first time the user uses the system, a *sign-up* portal is available; in case the user already has an account, then it may use their email, phone number, or unique-use code to *sign in*. Also, an OAuth-based alternative [29] is available.

Finally, the User Interface (UI) must be intuitive to the broadest demographic possible, given that the pet-owner profile differs significantly by both ethnicity [30] and age [31]. To that end, the `shadcdn` collection was employed to achieve a simple and consistent presentation. It allows for a quick design process, by simply selecting which UI elements to display. Furthermore, `TailwindCSS` was used to define the remaining styles, which easily integrates the previously mentioned components. For the programming language and framework, `TypeScript` and `Next.js` were chosen, respectively. `TypeScript` enhances the overall experience by enabling a static typing system, easing the integration process of the different elements in the system, and a streamlined refactoring routine. The `Node.js` framework, being `React`-based, provides Server-Side Rendering (SSR), ensuring the application is fast and adheres to the best Search engine optimization (SEO) practices [32], [33]. It also provides automatic code splitting, executing only the needed JavaScript for each page. This advocates a coding practice in which each page becomes a self-contained package, encapsulating its logic and state, and fostering scalability.

The connection between the backend and the frontend components of the Application layer is done through the `fetch` API to execute the requested methods and later display the retrieved responses as diverse visualizations (e.g., line graphs) implemented via the selected and imported components. This provides an interface that is tailored to the modules and submodules each user manages in its home environment, cohesively. It is also through this API that users interact securely with the authentication system.

## IV. Evaluation & Results

After designing and developing the complete solution, its applicability was tested through several use cases to assess how it behaves given different real-world conditions. It is of utmost importance that the solution is robust to the variability of the environment it may eventually be installed into, and that it can handle a vast array of different scenarios, proving the universal adaptability and appeal of the approach. However, given the experimental nature of this work, different testing scenarios were implemented using prototypes and scale models as a way to simulate likely circumstances where this solution may be inserted into, proving its practicability more abstractly. These test scenarios were based on a cat monitoring situation, thus comprising different cat care aspects. It should be noted that, based on the versatility of the approach, if the apparatus is applicable in a scale model of a given setting, then it should be, theoretically, also applicable in the circumstances it hopes to simulate.

As previously stated, end users can simply follow a short list of steps to get the solution running locally, by cloning the repository, and executing each component in a containerised manner, automatically. Given that the physical components are correctly connected (as we are leveraging prototype-oriented hardware), in theory, the solution should be able to correctly capture relevant environment data about activities carried out by the pet, or to the pet itself. In this sense, Figure 2 contains an example of a graph visualization accessible through the web application.

### A. Pet Monitoring

Room monitoring is an indirect but essential tracking method for pet care applications. To measure the temperature and humidity of the room, a tracking submodule was implemented, powered by a Temperature & Humidity Sensor. Furthermore, environmental healthiness is also measured through a Carbon Monoxide Sensor [34]. In addition to this, a live sound feed of the environment was achieved through a Sound Sensor [35], allowing the solution to register peaks of sound activity that could indicate distress calls. The application was able to display both environmental and sound activity through time-series graphs.

### B. Litter Box Activity

To test the applicability of a litter box activity tracking feature, a Soil Moisture Sensor [36] was employed. This sensor was placed inside a small box containing a common household brand of cat litter, which was watered periodically. The data throughput allowed the solution to create a visual representation of how moist the soil was at a given time, through a time-series graph, and effectively highlight litter box activity even through repeated usages in short periods. Moreover, a more elaborate testing procedure regarding this specific behaviour was set forth, in which the footage captured from a serial camera would be used in tandem with the previously mentioned sensor outputs as a way to verify litter occurrences in a multimodal manner. If the live feed displayed significant differences comparatively to a record of an empty litter box, this data could be cross-referenced with moisture sensor data to ensure a verifiable reading of activity.

### C. Automatic Pet Feeding

To simulate an automatic pet feeding feature, a Pressure Sensor [37] was utilized and tested against different levels of touch pressure to ascertain if the presence of the pet could be used as an indicator that food should be served. This mechanism could be subsequently implemented in tandem with a feeding actuator (e.g., a small motor connected to a food box door). The application was able to register touch activity and represent it in a time-series graph.

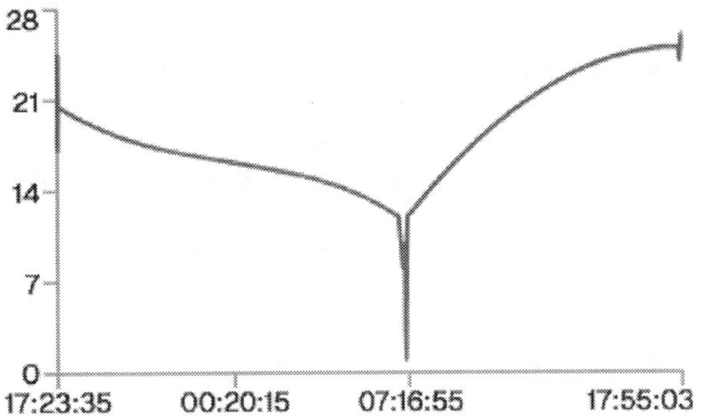


Figure 2. Simple graph visualization of the temperature in Celsius by time of day, present in the web application. Displays a sharp decline during nighttime.

## V. Discussion

Several potential benefits surfaced when implementing use cases based on the outlined proposal. As evidenced by the conclusions drawn from the assembled scenarios, Fursight is a rather adaptable system given its modular nature, which also contributes to its scalability factor, as shown by the successful construction of scale models, suggesting applicability in full-scale settings. Furthermore, this ease in implementing different arrangements showcased how streamlined the deployment process is even for end users, showcasing its possible adaptability in other contexts, such as pet hotels or veterinary clinics. In these cases, even against higher setup complexity, Fursight allows each client to manage their system comprehensively through the web application. The developed solution not only allows for multi-faceted and comprehensive monitoring of pet well-being but also permits doing it in real-time via easily interpretable visualizations. Additionally, the non-invasive nature of the solution was upheld throughout development, given that no appliance needed to be set directly on the pet.

Nonetheless, some shortcomings also came to light. Given the experimental nature of the solution, strict bounds were placed on the planned implementations, restraining their faithfulness to their real-world counterparts. For the same reason, a rigid emphasis is put on a correct physical setup. Moreover, since the devices used for the physical components stem from a prototypal nature, the showcased sensibility was sometimes inappropriate, as seen in the pressure sensor, which ought to be triggered by non-pet activities. Overall, although the practical value of the solution was showcased, it would not be a reasonable commercial solution in its current state.

## VI. Conclusion & Future Work

This project demonstrated a novel integrated solution for pet monitoring using IoT and CPS, called Fursight. This modular approach to pet care seamlessly integrates several sensors (and actuators) to monitor pets, alongside their involving environment, without the need to hook attachments to their bodies. The modular architecture, comprising physical, middleware, and application layers, allows for adaptive deployment in various home configurations. While promising results were produced during simulated experiments, several limitations surfaced, mainly due to the experimental nature of the setup.

For future work, given the modularity aspect of the solution, it would be beneficial to further integrate more complex submodules, such as making the live feed constantly and irrevocably available to the end user, while also enhancing accuracy in activity detection. In a commercial context, it would be best to provide a more streamlined setup process by devising a simpler integrated standalone service, combined with a more robust, sellable physical package, which could comprise diverse key components required for the full operational capability of the solution, as well as modular expansions for extra functionality. Ultimately, Fursight represents a robust solution to unobtrusive pet care, combining IoT and human-centred design, to reach optimal care even in the prevailing fast-paced mode of life.

## ACKNOWLEDGMENT

This work was financially supported by project openZDM – "Open Platform for Realizing Zero Defects in Cyber Physical Manufacturing" - GA nº. 101058673, funded by the European Commission under the Horizon Europe program. The authors gratefully acknowledge the support provided by the Foundation for Science and Technology (FCT/MCTES) within the scope of the Associated Laboratory ARISE (LA/P/0112/2020), and the R&D Unit SYSTEC through Base (UIDB/00147/2020) and Programmatic (UIDP/00147/2020) funds.

## REFERENCES

[1] K. J. Scoresby *et al.*, "Pet Ownership and Quality of Life: A Systematic Review of the Literature," *Veterinary Sciences*, vol. 8, no. 12, 2021, ISSN: 2306-7381. DOI: 10.3390/vetsci8120332.

[2] A. Mitek, D. Jones, A. Newell, and S. Vitale, "Wearable devices in veterinary health care," *Veterinary Clinics: Small Animal Practice*, vol. 52, no. 5, pp. 1087–1098, 2022.

[3] Y. Shenoda, M. P. Ward, D. McKeegan, and A. Fawcett, "The cone of shame: welfare implications of Elizabethan collar use on dogs and cats as reported by their owners," *Animals*, vol. 10, no. 2, p. 333, 2020.

[4] Y. Chen and M. Elshakankiri, "Implementation of an iot based pet care system," in *2020 Fifth International Conference on Fog and Mobile Edge Computing (FMEC)*, 2020, pp. 256–262. DOI: 10.1109/FMEC49853.2020.9144910.

[5] A. Santos *et al.*, "Fursight's Github Repository," [Online]. Available: https://github.com/FurSAIght/FurSight (visited on 01/14/2025).

[6] P. D. P. Adi *et al.*, "Optimization and Development of Raspberry Pi 4 Model B for the Internet of Things," in *2023 IEEE 9th Information Technology International Seminar (ITIS)*, IEEE, 2023, pp. 1–6.

[7] R. K. Kodali and A. Anjum, "IoT based home automation using node-red," in *2018 Second International Conference on Green Computing and Internet of Things (ICGCIoT)*, IEEE, 2018, pp. 386–390.

[8] J. Nickoloff and S. Kuenzli, *Docker in action*. Simon and Schuster, 2019.

[9] M. Tauseef, E. Rathod, S. M. Nandish, and M. G. Kushal, "Advancements in Pet Care Technology: A Comprehensive Survey," in *2024 4th International Conference on Data Engineering and Communication Systems (ICDECS)*, Mar. 2024, pp. 1–6. DOI: 10.1109/ICDECS59733.2023.10503555.

[10] S. Nithin Wilfred Reyu and J. Pearly Princess, "IoT based Pet Health Monitoring System for Sick Pets," in *2024 3rd International Conference on Applied Artificial Intelligence and Computing (ICAAIC)*, Jun. 2024, pp. 1648–1652. DOI: 10.1109/ICAAIC60222.2024.10574965.

[11] I. Rozlomii, A. Yarmilko, and S. Naumenko, "Data security of IoT devices with limited resources: challenges and potential solutions.," in *doors*, 2024, pp. 85–96.

[12] Y. Quiñonez, C. Lizarraga, R. Aguayo, and D. Arredondo, "Communication architecture based on IoT technology to control and monitor pets feeding," en, *JUCS - Journal of Universal Computer Science*, vol. 27, no. 2, pp. 190–207, Feb. 2021, ISSN: 0948-6968, 0948-695X. DOI: 10.3897/jucs.65094.

[13] W. P. Rey and K. W. J. D. Rey, "AZKALS: Revolutionizing pet care with an IoT-powered smart dog cage management system," in *2024 3rd International Conference on Computer Technologies (ICCTech)*, IEEE, 2024, pp. 48–54.

[14] J.-W. Kang and Y. Namkung, "The role of personalization on continuance intention in food service mobile apps: A privacy calculus perspective," *International Journal of Contemporary Hospitality Management*, vol. 31, no. 2, pp. 734–752, 2019.

[15] V. Prithviraj and K. Sriharipriya, "Smart Pet Feeder System Based on Google Assistant," in *2022 IEEE International Conference on Distributed Computing and Electrical Circuits and Electronics (ICDCECE)*, IEEE, 2022, pp. 1–6.

[16] M. Sharma and R. Gautam, "Evolving Pet Care Landscape: Exploring Digital Marketing, Educational Tech, and User Experience Trends," *Advances in Urban Resilience and Sustainable City Design*, vol. 14, no. 12, pp. 13–34, 2022.

[17] V. Cerf and R. Kahn, "A protocol for packet network intercommunication," *IEEE Transactions on communications*, vol. 22, no. 5, pp. 637–648, 1974.

[18] G. M. Roy, *RabbitMQ in depth*. Simon and Schuster, 2017.

[19] J. Mankar, C. Darode, K. Trivedi, M. Kanoje, and P. Shahare, "Review of I2C protocol," *International Journal of Research in Advent Technology*, vol. 2, no. 1, pp. 474–479, 2014.

[20] M. Alliance, "I3C," 2025, [Online]. Available: https://www.mipi.org/specifications/i3c-sensor-specification (visited on 01/15/2025).

[21] A. Meroth and P. Sora, "Serial Peripheral Interface (SPI)," in *Sensor networks in theory and practice: Successfully realize embedded systems projects*, Springer, 2023, pp. 205–224.

[22] A. Gupta and C. Charan, "Analysis of Universal Asynchronous Receiver-Transmitter (UART)," in *2024 2nd International Conference on Device Intelligence, Computing and Communication Technologies (DICCT)*, IEEE, 2024, pp. 194–198.

[23] O. Standard, "MQTT Version 5.0," *Retrieved June*, vol. 22, no. 2020, p. 1435, 2019.

[24] T. Stapko, "CHAPTER 2 - Network Communications Protocols and Built-in Security," in *Practical Embedded Security*, T. Stapko, Ed., Burlington: Newnes, 2008, pp. 23–48, ISBN: 978-0-7506-8215-2. DOI: https://doi.org/10.1016/B978-075068215-2.50003-3.

[25] W. McKinney, *Python for data analysis: Data wrangling with Pandas, NumPy, and IPython.* " O'Reilly Media, Inc.", 2012.

[26] A. G. M. Standard *et al.*, "Protocol Specification," *Network Programming, SunOS*, vol. 4, pp. 1–69, 2006.

[27] Supabase, "Build in a weekend. Scale to millions.," [Online]. Available: https://nodered.org/ (visited on 01/14/2025).

[28] M. Masse, *REST API design rulebook.* " O'Reilly Media, Inc.", 2011.

[29] R. Boyd, *Getting started with OAuth 2.0.* " O'Reilly Media, Inc.", 2012.

[30] J. W. Applebaum, C. W. Peek, and B. A. Zsembik, "Examining US pet ownership using the General Social Survey," *The Social Science Journal*, vol. 60, no. 1, pp. 110–119, 2023.

[31] N. R. Gee and M. K. Mueller, "A systematic review of research on pet ownership and animal interactions among older adults," *Anthrozoös*, vol. 32, no. 2, pp. 183–207, 2019.

[32] S. Holay, S. Wankhede, N. Gaikwad, and S. Tandekar, "Understanding When to Use SSR and CSR in Modern Web Development," *Journal of Technical Education*, p. 277, 2024.

[33] K. Vallamsetla, "The Impact of Server-Side Rendering on UI Performance and SEO," *International Journal of Scientific Research in Computer Science, Engineering and Information Technology*, vol. 10, no. 5, pp. 795–804, 2024.

[34] H. E. G. Corporation, "Technical Data MQ-7 Gas Sensor," 2004, [Online]. Available: https://www.sparkfun.com/datasheets/Sensors/Biometric/MQ-7.pdf (visited on 01/14/2025).

[35] ArduinoModules.info, "KY-037 High Sensitivity Sound Detection Module," [Online]. Available: https://arduinomodules.info/ky-037-high-sensitivity-sound-detection-module/ (visited on 01/14/2025).

[36] DFRobot, "Gravity: Analog Soil Moisture Sensor for Arduino and Raspberry Pi (SKU: SEN0114)," [Online]. Available: https://www.dfrobot.com/product-599.html (visited on 01/14/2025).

[37] DFRobot, "DFRobot Capacitive Touch Sensor (SKU: DFR0030)," [Online]. Available: https://wiki.dfrobot.com/DFRobot%5C_Capacitive%5C_Touch%5C_Sensor%5C_SKU%5C_DFR0030 (visited on 01/14/2025).

# Automation of Beer Dispensers: A Cyber-Physical System Solution

Lorenzo Piarulli[1,4], Luca Di Pietro[1,3], José A. Gaspar[1], Miguel A. Teixeira[1], Jaume Sansano[1,5], Lucas Sousa[1], Luís Paiva[1], Emanuel Gestosa[1], Alexandre Correia[1], Rui Pinto[1,2], Gil Gonçalves[1,2]
Dept. of Informatics Engineering Faculty of Engineering, University of Porto, Porto, Portugal[1]
SYSTEC, ARISE, Faculty of Engineering, University of Porto, Porto, Portugal[2]
Dept. of Computer Science Engineering Polytechnic University of Milan, Milan, Italy[3]
Dept. of Computer Science Engineering Sapienza University of Rome, Rome, Italy[4]
Dept. of Informatics Engineering Polytechnic University of Valencia, Valencia, Spain[5]
Email: {up202401433, up202401432, up202008561, up202005208, up202402362, up202004682, up202006094, up202005485, up202007042}@up.pt
{rpinto, gil}@fe.up.pt

***Abstract*—This study explores the implementation of Internet of Things technology to improve drink service and management in local establishments. Current alternatives were analyzed but failed to satisfy all the problem's requirements, leading us to propose a new solution. Our system uses a mobile application that allows users to purchase beer tokens, which can be uploaded to establishment cups using Near Field Communication (NFC) technology. Once the cup contains a token, it can interact with a prototype self-serving tank that dispenses the drink upon validation by the client. The app also provides real-time updates on tank temperature and level for the owner. A key consideration during the design phase was ensuring the architecture's scalability to handle multiple interactions between devices. The successful development of our prototype demonstrates the feasibility of implementing this technology in real-world establishments, highlighting its market potential. Finally, we analyzed the product's limitations and proposed directions for future research and development.**

***Keywords*-*Internet of Things; Cyber-Physical Systems; self-service; service tank; automation.***

## I. Introduction

In recent years, there has been growing interest in the Internet of Things (IoT) [1] in fields such as personal goods, transportation, and industry due to the advances in technology and the promising results of its implementation [2]. IoT and Cyber-Physical Systems (CPS) [3] are expected to take a major role in future production value chains by using networks of sensors and actuators to gather data.

A critical challenge in the service sector is the inefficiency caused by human limitations. Nowadays, it is common for establishments to face a simultaneous high demand when dealing with traditional staff systems. The growing acceptance of self-serving devices [4] encourages big companies to implement similar technologies in areas, such as gas stations or supermarkets, removing the human factor of the cashiers. This change of mentality could be extended through other consumer sectors such as bar service. This study aims to address these challenges by developing a self-serving beer dispenser powered by IoT and CPS. The primary objectives of this work are to reduce waiting times, improve customer experience, and provide real-time data insights to establishment owners for better resource management.

Our solution consists of using IoT to create a self-serving tank that allows the user through their phone to purchase, validate, and receive a drink without the need for a member of staff. The user uses NFC tags attached to the cups to load tokens purchased via our phone app, then they can walk to the tank, validate that they want to use the token and receive a drink. This removes the necessity of a staff member and optimizes the service process and makes it more dynamic. To provide insights to the owner we can also measure in real-time values of the tank's level and temperature to ensure uninterrupted service. The resulting product could help an establishment to have a better understanding of its resources and promote a more direct service to the customers focusing on reducing waiting time and cost.

The remaining sections are arranged as follows: Section II reviews the most relevant related works in the field of automated beverage dispensing systems, highlighting their limitations. Section III describes the proposed solution, including its design, architecture, and main components. Section IV presents the results obtained and evaluates the performance of the prototype. Section V discusses the advantages, limitations, and potential improvements of the system. Finally, Section VI concludes the paper by summarizing the main contributions and possible future changes.

## II. Related Work

Efforts to enhance efficiency, automation, and user experience in beverage dispensing have spurred the development of various smart beer dispensing systems, each with distinct strengths and limitations [5]. The Pubinno Smart Tap [6] exemplifies the use of artificial intelligence to optimize beer quality by fine-tuning temperature and pressure levels. Despite these innovations, its reliance on proprietary kegs and the absence of self-service features may hinder its accessibility. A staff-centric application accompanies the system, offering tools for monitoring performance.

PourMyBeer [7], by contrast, empowers patrons with self-service capabilities using Radio Frequency Identification (RFID) technology, simplifying transactions and providing valuable sales insights for operators. While compatible with standard kegs, the system lacks real-time authentication and quality assurance features. Similarly, Boxbar Tech [8] provides automated self-service kiosks designed to minimize wait times and boost service speed. Although the kiosks support standard kegs, they do not specialize in beer-specific features, such as temperature control, but include an app for inventory and sales oversight.

Another self-service solution, the iPourIt system [9], grants users access to a variety of beverages while enabling real-time data monitoring. However, its limitations lie in security and centralized control integration, although it offers operators tools for live system configuration and data oversight. Heineken SmartDispense [10], on the other hand, prioritizes beer quality through advanced cooling and line management techniques, promoting sustainability. Yet, it lacks self-service functionality and real-time monitoring, while relying on proprietary kegs. Its accompanying application focuses on staff support, tracking temperature and cleaning schedules.

These systems highlight diverse approaches, emphasizing either quality assurance, operational efficiency, or self-service functionality. However, they often fall short of addressing comprehensive needs, such as robust security, authentication, and user-centric innovation. This analysis underscores the potential for future systems to bridge these gaps and adapt to evolving demands in the industry.

## III. Proposed Solution

In the following sections, we present the implemented architecture, which follows the prototype illustrated in Figure 1. Our solution aims to enhance transaction security for commercial purposes. As shown in the scheme, when the user initiates liquid pouring from the tank, several steps must be completed. First, the user generates a token in the application, which is then transmitted to the cup and subsequently to the tank. The tank verifies the token with the cloud, which sends a confirmation request to the user. The pouring system starts only after the cloud confirms the token and the user accepts the request.

### A. Hardware

The hardware aspect of this project incorporates two types of microcontrollers: the Arduino Nano WiFi [11] and the Raspberry Pi 4 Model B (2GB) [12], as represented in Figure 2.

The Raspberry Pi serves as an Edge server, managing local communication between the automated tanks. The system is designed so that each shop equipped with automated beer dispensing tanks has an Edge server (in this case, the Raspberry Pi implementation) to oversee all associated tanks. Each tank automation system employs an Arduino for its operations. Thus, every shop has multiple Arduino-based systems connected to the shop's Raspberry Pi, which centralizes and handles communications.

The Arduino system is responsible for monitoring the system, sending data, detecting RFID cup tokens, and pouring the correct amount of beer. It serves as the central controller for the beer dispensing system. The initial prototype was

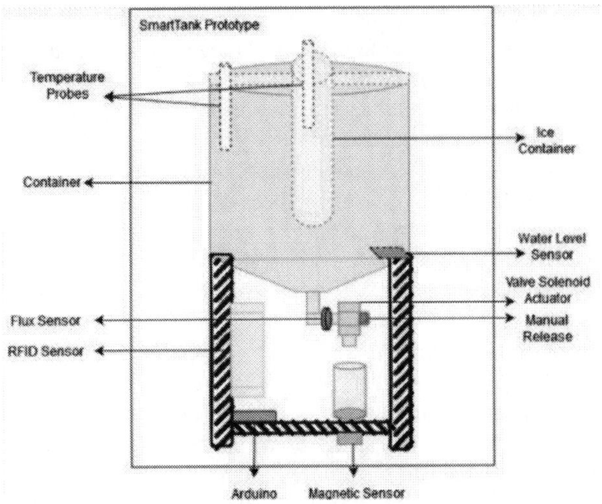


Figure 1. Overview of the system's proof of concept.

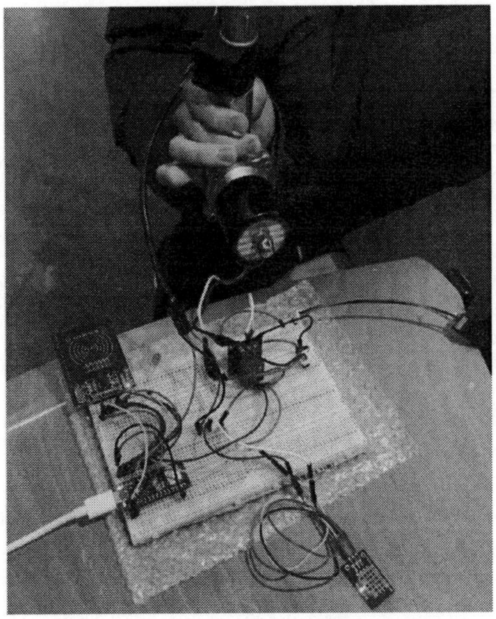

Figure 2. Hardware system with all the components.

built using an Arduino Uno, which lacks WiFi capabilities. After verifying the electronic circuit and achieving a working prototype, we transitioned to the Arduino Nano WiFi to enable seamless communication for data transmission and the inclusion of token validation features. Regarding the electronics, the circuit integrates the following sensors and actuators: I) RFID Reader (RFID-RC522) with associated tags; II) Humidity and Temperature Sensor (DHT11); III) Relay Module(JQC3F-5VDC-C); IV) Flux Sensor (Youmile YF-S201); V) Solenoid Valve (BACOENG B06XFD1CB4); VI) 12 V Charger; VII) Diode; VIII) Resistors and cables.

The system starts by identifying a user's RFID-equipped cup, using the RFID Token Detection. The token, preloaded via a mobile application, is transmitted from the cup's RFID tag to the Arduino through the RFID reader. Once the token is read, the Arduino requests validation from the central system and awaits confirmation. After validation, the Arduino signals the relay to activate the solenoid valve. The relay connects the valve to the 12V power supply, allowing the valve to open. With the valve open, the beer dispensing starts, i.e., the liquid begins to flow. The flux sensor (Youmile YF-S201 [13]) measures the volume of fluid dispensed in millilitres. Once the desired amount of beer is dispensed, the Arduino closes the valve and resets the flow status.

The system employs a solenoid valve activated by a relay, which requires a higher voltage than the Arduino's output. The relay is controlled by a 3.3V signal from the Arduino, allowing the solenoid to open and regulate liquid flow, with pressure maintenance ensuring proper functionality. Liquid flow is monitored by a sensor that generates pulses, which the Arduino processes to calculate volume after calibration for accuracy.

Both the solenoid valve and flow sensor feature commercial connectors for easy replacement and adaptation, supporting future upgrades. The system provides staff with key metrics like liquid volume and temperature, with a DHT11 sensor measuring temperature and humidity at adjustable intervals. Data is sent to a Raspberry Pi, which forwards it to the Cloud for monitoring.

Finally, the Firmware, developed using the Arduino IDE in C/C++, integrates RFID, sensor, and actuator control. Despite the Arduino's single-process nature, interrupt-based programming ensures efficient task management and continuous data collection without disruption. The modular code structure supports easy updates and the addition of new features.

### B. Communication

The communication part of the project aims to define a scalable architecture for the network and the best communication protocols to go along with it. The chosen architecture is detailed in Figure 3. The overall topology of the network follows a star topology, with a Message Queuing Telemetry Transport (MQTT) [14] broker in the central hub. The communication protocols used are Hyper Text Transfer Protocol Secure (HTTPS) and MQTT.

Transitioning to Edge Computing or Decentralized Communication presents several challenges, including high infrastructure costs, complex management, and security risks due to increased attack surfaces. Ensuring data synchronization and consistency across distributed tanks is difficult, especially with limited computing power and connectivity issues. Software updates, interoperability, and failure handling require robust solutions, while compliance with regulatory standards can be complex without centralized control. Despite these challenges, edge computing offers lower latency, enhanced privacy, and reduced cloud dependency, making it a promising but demanding shift. Based on these facts, we have decided to build an architecture that leverages the benefits of both edge computing and the cloud.

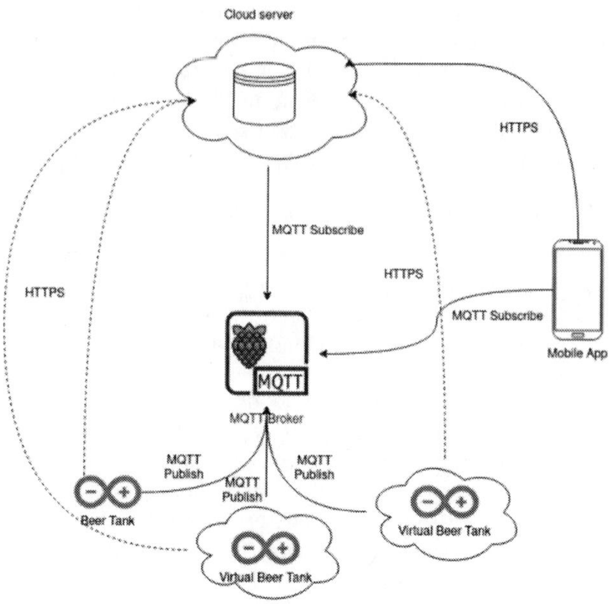


Figure 3. Overview of the system's components and their communication.

The Beer Tanks are the Edge devices, and the MQTT broker is in the same network as them, acting as a Fog layer, bridging the Edge to the Cloud layer. The MQTT protocol is used to publish sensor data from the Edge devices and to subscribe to it from the Cloud and the mobile application, where the raw data is processed and visualized.

The HTTPS protocol is used for mobile application to Cloud communication, and also for some sporadic communication between the Edge devices and the Cloud. This means that the Edge devices may bypass the Fog layer and communicate directly to the Cloud, but this is only done for purposes of validating beer tokens. This type of validation is done by sending a request for validation and waiting for a response, therefore using MQTT, which follows a publish-subscriber paradigm, for this type of communication made no sense, hence why we allow the use of HTTPS, which follows a request-response paradigm, in this specific case.

While in Figure 3 we presented an architecture with the MQTT broker as the central hub, we still accounted for the possibility of scaling the system for having multiple brokers with just minimal adjustment. Since the Edge devices and the MQTT broker are situated on the same network, they are meant to all be in the same establishment, i.e., the place that sells the beer to the public. Therefore, to scale for multiple establishments, each one of them would have their own Edge devices and their MQTT broker, and all of them would communicate with the Cloud.

### C. Cloud

The objective of the API is to provide logic to the business. It supports secure client login, real-time tracking of tank parameters, data offload, and logic processing to provide better implementation of the app. Provides features such as the management of organizations, tanks, and human resources, as well as token management and key performance indicator systems.

The structure of the API's database consists of the models for establishments, users, tokens and tanks. Establishment models contain details about the bar which are used in the user model for login and access to other functionalities. Tokens are a multipurpose means that allows the user to exchange them for a drink from a particular machine, they link a user to a machine to an organization. There are other related models attached to tanks, which determine the amount of beer, its temperature and its history of consumption. The database is structured with normalized relational models to efficiently manage data integrity across entities. Advanced relationships between models, such as the many-to-many mapping of users and establishments via the *EstablishmentStaff* model, enable precise role-based access control and granular permission management. Additionally, the system supports dynamic endpoint handling, enabling contextual validation for complex workflows like token verification.

The API's endpoints handle a variety of tasks. User authentication endpoints enable registration, login, and auth token refreshing. The establishment management endpoints allow users to create establishments and retrieve related tanks or tokens. The token endpoints support the creation, updates, and verification of tokens. The staff endpoints retrieve the personnel details for the establishments. Statistics endpoints provide real-time data on tank performance, such as beer served, temperature, and levels, as well as aggregated data for establishments. Admin-specific endpoints allow access to all users and establishments for high-level management.

The API is deployed on Render.com with an automated system that pushes changes to production after every code commit. Security is ensured by requiring JavaScript Object Notation (JSON) Web Tokens (JWT) for all secure endpoints, with role-based access control distinguishing between admin and regular user permissions. This API serves as a scalable backend solution for managing self-service beer pouring systems. It combines secure user management, comprehensive data tracking, and analytics into a single service, ensuring ease of use.

### D. Security

This project addressed several non-functional security requirements to ensure the system's robustness, such as Token Protection; Communication Flow; Secure Communication Protocols; Server Security; Internal Network Security; and Physical Security.

To prevent misuse of a stolen cup loaded with a beer token, a confirmation feature was implemented. When the user places the cup near the NFC sensor, a request is sent to the application for confirmation. The user must approve the request via the application's confirmation page to activate the machine and spend the token. This two-step process ensures only the rightful token owner can use the machine.

The hardware sends a confirmation request to the Cloud, and the application polls the Cloud to retrieve pending confirmations. Upon user approval, the information is sent back through the Cloud to the machine. While direct communication between the application and hardware would be more efficient, the Cloud was used as an intermediary because it verifies token validity and manages user confirmations.

Ensuring secure communication between system components is critical. All communication uses cryptographic protocols, such as HTTPS instead of HTTP, and MQTT over Transport Layer Security (TLS) [15]. Additionally, since MQTT does not enforce authentication by default, the system was configured to require strong, randomly generated passwords for authentication.

Remote management of servers introduces additional security considerations. For Cloud servers, security largely depends on the provider, but standard practices, such as using strong passwords, are essential. For Fog servers, owned and managed by the system operator, secure deployment and regular updates are critical to minimizing vulnerabilities.

In the beer establishment, where Edge and Fog devices operate, network security is crucial. The Fog device, serving as the MQTT broker, must be accessible from the Internet. To secure this setup, the Fog device should be placed in a demilitarized zone (DMZ) [16] with a firewall separating it from the Edge devices. This configuration mitigates potential risks to the internal network.

Edge devices are also vulnerable to physical attacks, whether by malicious users attempting to obtain free beer or accidental damage. Implementing robust hardware security measures is as important as addressing cyber threats.

In terms of non-functional requirements, this project took into account a few security concerns. The first one is the possibility of a stolen cup, with a loaded beer token in it. To avoid someone else, other than the token owner, to activate the machine, a confirmation feature was implemented. The idea is that, upon activation, this is, when the user passes the cup near the NFC sensor of the machine, a request is sent to the application in the form of a confirmation. The user must go to the confirmation page, in the application, and confirm that the user wants to use the machine with that token. Only if the user accepts the confirmation, the machine is activated and the token is spent. In terms of implementation, the hardware sends the request to the Cloud, and on the application side, a polling system is done to get the latest confirmations. Upon user confirmation, the information goes through the Cloud again and arrives at the machine. This solution is not optimal, it would be more efficient if the communication was directly made between the application and hardware, however, the Cloud was the only element that checked for token validity and it was also responsible for getting all confirmations for a given user.

Providing secure communications between the components of the system is also a critical requirement. Communication protocols should always use cryptographic enhancements to achieve security properties. Therefore, HTTPS is always used instead of HTTP, and MQTT is also used on top of TLS [15]. Also, MQTT by default doesn't require any authentication, so we had to configure it to require authentication using a strong, randomly generated password.

We also consider that it is desirable to have the servers, both on the Fog and the Cloud layers, be remotely managed. With that comes more security implications. For the Cloud, it will depend mostly on the Cloud provider, but standard security practices, such as choosing strong passwords, still apply. For the Fog layer, since it is controlled by the owner of the system, one has to be very careful to deploy it without security flaws and keep it properly updated.

### E. Application

A mobile app was chosen over a web app for its convenience and user-friendly interface. The app allows users at establishments equipped with dispensing machines to view, use, and purchase tokens easily. For staff, it provides real-time and historical insights into beer tank metrics, such as temperature and beer levels, which are crucial for optimizing operations and boosting profitability. Development and Security

The application is developed using Flutter [17], ensuring cross-platform compatibility. It includes user-centred features such as login, registration, and session management. A session extension mechanism minimizes the need for frequent logins. Upon login, users receive two tokens: I) Bearer Token: Used for secure requests to the Cloud and automatically refreshed when invalid; II) Refresh Token: Enables the generation of new bearer and refresh tokens. If the refresh token expires (less frequently), the user must log in again.

Users can generate beer tokens for specific establishments, initialized with the status *"Phone"*. Tokens are listed in the app and, when selected, can be loaded into an NFC-equipped cup. The app uses the phone's NFC module to write the token, changing its status to *"Cup"* and syncing this update with the Cloud. The NFC writing process uses Flutter's NFC Manager package [18], encoding the token as a 4-digit integer in the NFC Data Exchange Format (NDEF) [19]. Also, the app displays each establishment's tanks and total beer servings. Detailed metrics, such as beer level and temperature, are available for individual tanks. Historical data is visualized through graphs created using the FL Chart [20] package, enabling better decision-making and operational efficiency.

Regarding real-time data, Beer tank metrics (temperature and level) are collected via an MQTT channel from the establishment's Raspberry Pi using the Pub/Sub protocol. This ensures immediate updates for the app. There are also historical data, pre-processed in the Cloud and retrieved via an API. This is formatted for visualization on the app, reducing client-side processing overhead.

Finally, an API wrapper was developed to streamline communication with the Cloud. Although not a core feature, it significantly simplifies app development. All communication uses secure POST and GET HTTPS requests, protected by bearer tokens.

## IV. Validation and Result Analysis

In this section, we present the methods used to test our automated beer dispensing system, discuss the experimental setup and analyze the outcomes to demonstrate the system's effectiveness and feasibility.

### A. Testing Methodology

To verify the functionality, performance, and reliability of our automated beer dispenser, we established the following testing methodology:

- **Functional Tests:** We examined the basic features (e.g., token validation, solenoid valve control, flow sensor readings) in a controlled environment. Each feature was tested independently, and success/failure logs were recorded.
- **Integration Tests:** Once the individual modules were verified, we tested the entire workflow from token creation on the mobile application to the final dispensation of beer. This aimed to spot any synchronization or communication issues among the Arduino, Raspberry Pi, mobile application, and the Cloud.

### B. Result Analysis

Through our tests, we confirmed that the prototype is both functional and robust, successfully meeting the specified performance objectives in terms of reliability, scalability and security. Figure 4 shows the final results on the application side. Note that the data displayed in these figures are mocked values rather than actual sensor readings. Nonetheless, the sensors were fully tested and confirmed to be working correctly during firmware development.

## V. Discussion

The development and implementation of the automated beer dispensing system aim to address periods of high demand and labour shortages by providing an efficient, self-service solution. The system offers several advantages that enhance its overall effectiveness and adaptability. By streamlining the beverage-dispensing process, it reduces waiting times and improves the customer experience. Operational efficiency is significantly increased as the system automates repetitive tasks, allowing staff to focus on enhancing service quality. The integration of cloud infrastructure enables real-time monitoring and analysis of operational data, providing valuable insights into customer behaviour and resource management. Security is strengthened through NFC tokens and confirmation systems, which restrict access to authorized users only. Moreover, the system's modularity and scalability allow for easy upgrades and adaptations to evolving operational needs, while proper customization can help minimize waste, optimize resource utilization, and promote sustainability. However, despite these advantages, the system faces several limitations that impact its performance and usability. Communication latency, due to reliance on cloud hosts for token validation and confirmation, may lead to delays that affect the user experience in high-demand scenarios. Hardware constraints, particularly the single-threaded nature of the Arduino, limit its ability to

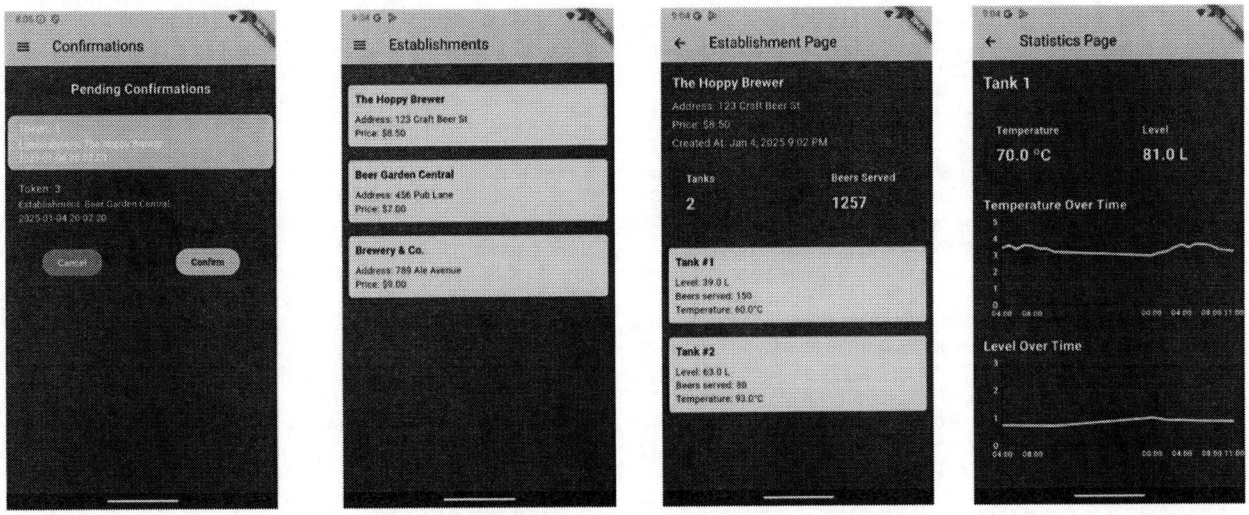


Figure 4. Confirmations, establishments and statistics screens.

handle multiple concurrent operations, potentially affecting real-time performance. The solenoid valve's dependency on stable liquid pressure makes it less reliable under varying conditions. Additionally, users unfamiliar with NFC technology or app-based interactions may initially find the system less intuitive, affecting adoption rates. While digital security is robust, the potential for physical theft of RFID cups remains a concern. Despite these challenges, the system presents a promising solution with opportunities for further improvement and optimization.

Addressing some of those limitations would not compensate the additional cost required to solve them. Examples of those improvements would be the usage of a more robust valve in terms of pressure, which will make the prototype suitable for most liquids, usage of hardware devices that support multi-threading and new hardware devices used in Edge computing to avoid reliance on the Cloud. The solution has been built for easy actuator and sensor replacement, allowing the system to adapt to new solutions that require automated tanks, like for agricultural or industrial applications.

## VI. Conclusion & Future Work

Using IoT, mobile app and other automation hardware, the automated beer dispensing system built in this project shows that we can overcome some of the operational bottlenecks in beverage service in general. The system shows great promise in increasing customer satisfaction and operational efficiency by enabling self-service capabilities, reducing wait time and providing real-time data insights. Due to the modular nature of the design, it can be scaled and adapted to various use cases, making it a versatile solution.

In the future, we will continue to improve the system architecture by trying Edge computing or decentralized communication models to avoid reliance on the Cloud. To improve real-time responsiveness and multitasking capabilities, hardware upgrades, including the use of multithreaded microcontrollers, will also be explored. Machine learning algorithms could also be integrated for predictive maintenance and dynamic adaptation based on user behaviour. In addition, features such as the implementation of different cup sizes and the consideration of the beer supplier as an actor in the system will be introduced. This will allow the system to automatically order beer from the supplier when the bar runs out, ensuring seamless operation. Lastly, usability improvements will be made based on user feedback, keeping the system intuitive and accessible to a wider audience. These improvements could make the automated beer dispensing system a groundbreaking innovation in the service sector.

## Acknowledgment

This work is financially supported by national funds through the FCT/MCTES (PIDDAC), under the Associate Laboratory Advanced Production and Intelligent Systems – ARISE LA/P/0112/2020 (DOI 10.54499/LA/P/0112/2020) and the Base Funding (UIDB/00147/2020) and Programmatic Funding (UIDP/00147/2020) of the R&D Unit Center for Systems and Technologies – SYSTEC.

## References

[1] D. Raggett, "W3c plans for developing standards for open markets of services for the iot: The internet of things (ubiquity symposium)," *Ubiquity*, vol. 2015, no. October, pp. 1–8, 2015.

[2] E. Borgia, "The internet of things vision: Key features, applications and open issues," *Computer Communications*, vol. 54, pp. 1–31, 2014, ISSN: 0140-3664. DOI: https://doi.org/10.1016/j.comcom.2014.09.008.

[3] R. Rajkumar, I. Lee, L. Sha, and J. Stankovic, "Cyber-physical systems: The next computing revolution," in *Design Automation Conference*, 2010, pp. 731–736. DOI: 10.1145/1837274.1837461.

[4] M. L. Meuter, A. L. Ostrom, R. I. Roundtree, and M. J. Bitner, "Self-service technologies: Understanding customer satisfaction with technology-based service encounters," *Journal of marketing*, vol. 64, no. 3, pp. 50–64, 2000.

[5] S. Violino, S. Figorilli, C. Costa, and F. Pallottino, "Internet of beer: A review on smart technologies from mash to pint," *Foods*, vol. 9, no. 7, p. 950, 2020.

[6] Pubinno, *Smart Tap: AI-powered Beer Dispensing System*, https://pubinno.com/smart-tap/, [Accessed: January 9, 2025], 2025.

[7] PourMyBeer, *Self-Pour Tap System*, https://pourmybeer.com/, [Accessed: January 9, 2025], 2025.

[8] Boxbar Tech, *Automated Self-Serve Bar Terminals*, https://www.boxbar.live/, [Accessed: January 9, 2025], 2025.

[9] iPourIt, *Self-Pour Beverage System*, https://ipouritinc.com/, [Accessed: January 9, 2025], 2025.

[10] HEINEKEN, *SmartDispense: Draught Beer Dispense System*, https://smartdispense.heineken.co.uk/, [Accessed: January 9, 2025], 2025.

[11] H. Al-Mimi, A. Al-Dahoud, M. Fezari, and M. S. Daoud, "A study on new arduino nano board for wsn and iot applications," *International Journal of Advanced Science and Technology*, vol. 29, no. 4, pp. 10 223–10 230, 2020.

[12] H. D. Ghael, L. Solanki, and G. Sahu, "A review paper on raspberry pi and its applications," *International Journal of Advances in Engineering and Management (IJAEM)*, vol. 2, no. 12, p. 4, 2020.

[13] Mauser, *Youmile YF-S201*, https://mauser.pt/catalog/product_info.php?products_id=095-0376, [Accessed: January 13, 2025], 2025.

[14] M. Bender, E. Kirdan, M.-O. Pahl, and G. Carle, "Open-source mqtt evaluation," in *2021 IEEE 18th Annual Consumer Communications & Networking Conference (CCNC)*, IEEE, 2021, pp. 1–4.

[15] P. V. A. Alexandre Urzhumtsev and P. D. Adams, "Tls from fundamentals to practice," *Crystallography Reviews*, vol. 19, no. 4, pp. 230–270, 2013. DOI: 10.1080/0889311X.2013.835806. eprint: https://doi.org/10.1080/0889311X.2013.835806.

[16] J. Crichigno, E. Bou-Harb, and N. Ghani, "A comprehensive tutorial on science dmz," *IEEE Communications Surveys & Tutorials*, vol. 21, no. 2, pp. 2041–2078, 2019. DOI: 10.1109/COMST.2018.2876086.

[17] M. L. Napoli, *Beginning flutter: a hands on guide to app development*. John Wiley & Sons, 2019.

[18] S. Ghosh, J. Goswami, A. Kumar, and A. Majumder, "Issues in nfc as a form of contactless communication: A comprehensive survey," in *2015 International Conference on Smart Technologies and Management for Computing, Communication, Controls, Energy and Materials (ICSTM)*, IEEE, 2015, pp. 245–252.

[19] S. Hameed, U. M. Jamali, and A. Samad, "Integrity protection of ndef message with flexible and enhanced nfc signature records," in *2015 IEEE Trustcom/BigDataSE/ISPA*, IEEE, vol. 1, 2015, pp. 368–375.

[20] J. Nanavati, S. Patel, U. Patel, and A. Patel, "Critical review and fine-tuning performance of flutter applications," in *2024 5th International Conference on Mobile Computing and Sustainable Informatics (ICMCSI)*, IEEE, 2024, pp. 838–841.

# SmartPool: An Automated CPS-Based System for Real-Time Water Quality Management

André Ávila[1], André C. Costa[1], André Soares[1], Daniel Rodrigues[1], Eduardo T. Ramos[1], João Alves[1], João C. Matos[1], Lourenço Gonçalves[1], Luís Cabral[1], Marco Rocha[1] Rui Pinto[1,2], Gil Gonçalves[1,2]
Dept. of Informatics Engineering, Faculty of Engineering, University of Porto, Porto, Portugal[1]
SYSTEC, ARISE, Faculty of Engineering, University of Porto, Porto, Portugal[2]
Email: {up202006767, up201905916, up202004161, up202006562, up201906732, up202007614, up202006280, up202004816, up202006464, up202004891}@up.pt
{rpinto, gil}@fe.up.pt

***Abstract*—Maintaining optimal water quality in swimming pools is critical for ensuring safety, hygiene, and user comfort. Traditional methods often rely on manual and regular adjustments, which are time-consuming, prone to errors, and operationally inefficient. External factors can lead to excessive maintenance and unnecessary water waste, while under-maintenance could result in cloudy, discoloured, and dirty water. This research presents a SmartPool Internet of Things (IoT)-based solution that automates the maintenance and management of water quality using integrated sensors and actuators. The pool system measures parameters, such as pH, chloride, temperature, and water levels to preserve and control aesthetic and health parameters. The solution provides real-time data visualization and user interaction through a user-friendly dashboard and supports automated decisions. The developed prototype solution consists of a minimum-value product version of the presented architecture centred on a Raspberry Pi that incorporates camera and recognition algorithms to enhance pool safety, physical assets, a web interface, and a middleware open-source solution. This work demonstrates how Internet of Things and Cyber-Physical Systems technologies can automate pool parameter management by ensuring sustainability and improving efficient operations.**

***Keywords*-Pool System; Pool Maintenance; Automation; Control; Asset Administration Shell**

## I. Introduction

Swimming pools have become an essential amenity in modern society, serving diverse purposes ranging from recreation and exercise to hospitality and tourism. As the number of pool users increases, the demand for efficient and safe pool management systems in private and public pools has also increased, due to growing health awareness, technological advancements, and cost efficiency [1]. Poor water conditions can lead to health hazards, such as skin irritations, eye discomfort, and the spread of waterborne diseases (Angdresey et al. [2]), underscoring the critical importance of effective pool maintenance.

Traditional pool maintenance practices typically involve manual and routine adjustments to address water quality imbalances. These methods are labor-intensive, time-consuming, and susceptible to human error, making them less than optimal. Additionally, they depend heavily on field operators, which can result in significant costs—posing challenges for pool owners with limited budgets [1].

In today's smart technology era, the Internet of Things (IoT), Cyber-Physical Systems (CPS), and Digital Twins (DTs), as industrial-technological enablers, present an opportunity to transform traditional pool management into a more automated and data-driven process [3]. By integrating advanced sensors and actuators with a central control and processing unit leveraging IoT Machine-to-Machine (M2M) connectivity, the system can continuously collect and process insights from the environment, as described in Kaur, Mishra, and Maheshwari [4]. Leveraging the implementation of DTs, asset's digital counterparts, the solution presented in this study enables advanced monitoring, analysis, and control throughout the lifecycle of systems or products [5].

This paper presents the development and implementation of a five-level architecture CPS-enabled solution for the SmartPool system, aimed at addressing the challenges of traditional pool maintenance. The primary objective of this work is to enhance the efficiency, sustainability, and safety of pool management systems. By integrating automation and real-time monitoring, the SmartPool system reduces reliance on manual interventions, minimizes operational costs, and improves water quality control. However, as this study represents a prototype, it presents certain limitations related to security, performance, and hardware, further discussed in Sections V and VI.

Concerning the structure, the remainder of this document is organized as follows: Section II provides a review of the related work in industrial solutions for pool management and a discussion of the outcomes, methodologies used, and gaps for innovation. Section III describes the methods and architecture of the proposed system. Section IV presents the results of the experiments and evaluations. Section V discusses the implications of this solution, along with limitations and potential improvements. Finally, Section VI concludes the paper and highlights directions for future research.

## II. Related Work

The evolution of IoT technologies has transformed swimming pool management by creating intelligent systems that go beyond traditional maintenance approaches. Modern smart pool systems integrate advanced sensors, communication technologies, and data analytics to provide comprehensive monitoring, safety, and efficiency solutions.

Recent research has demonstrated significant advances in real-time water quality monitoring. Hamid et al. [6] proposed a Smart Water Quality Monitoring System (SWQMS) that can automatically track critical parameters, such as pH levels and water temperature. The study revealed that while the time of day influences water temperature, it does not significantly impact pH levels, highlighting the importance of continuous monitoring. The work developed by Lakshmikantha et al. [7] further expanded this concept by creating a prototype that can measure multiple parameters, including temperature, pH, turbidity, water level, and water flow. Their system successfully demonstrated the ability to detect issues across different water sources, from swimming pools to industrial wastewater.

Safety remains a critical concern in pool management. The Smart Swimming Pool Management System (SSPMS) proposed by Sangeetha et al. [8] integrates ultrasonic and Passive Infrared (PIR) sensors to detect potential drowning incidents. The system can automatically activate an alarm and initiate water drainage procedures, representing a significant leap in proactive safety mechanisms. Building on this approach, Raj et al. [9] presented an enhanced system that not only detects drowning individuals but also monitors additional parameters, such as water temperature, water level, and the presence of intoxicated individuals. Their solution includes an ESP32-CAM module for image analysis and can send emergency notifications to rescue teams.

Underwater communication presents unique technological challenges. A recent study investigated IoT-LoRa technology for underwater applications, revealing that water type and turbidity significantly impact signal transmission. This research showed that swimming pool water provides the best signal characteristics, while seawater presents the most challenging environment for communication [10].

The work of Gloria, Cercas and Souto [11] demonstrated the potential of IoT gateway systems in creating smart environments. Their approach utilized a Raspberry Pi as an aggregation node and an Arduino as a sensor node, communicating through the MQTT protocol. This architecture provides a flexible framework for remote monitoring and control of pool environments. These Edge hardware can be combined with the Cloud for extra storage and computational analysis.

Swimming pool-related studies presented in the literature often shift the focus to the drowning problem and their solution into prevention and monitoring systems [9], and forget about the tons of diseases that poor water quality brings to pool users every year. The reviewed studies highlight key challenges, potential areas for improvement, and solutions aimed at enhancing automation and improving the quality of life for swimming pool users [12]. Building on these insights, this study introduces an innovative, state-of-the-art solution that leverages the implementation of Asset Administration Shells (AAS) using the open-source Eclipse BaSyx middleware [13].

## III. SmartPool Solution

The proposed solution incorporates an open-source middleware platform that utilizes an Asset Administration Shell [14], a standardized representation of a DT with uniform interfaces. This approach enables seamless control of the physical twin through bidirectional communication, facilitating real-time monitoring and adjustments. The implementation ensures horizontal scalability, allowing for the easy integration of additional devices. It also offers adaptability for deployment at the Edge [15] or within Fog computing [16] levels, along with robust interoperability, supporting a wide range of communication and data protocols.

The system includes an intuitive web-based User Interface (UI) that displays over-time metrics through a dashboard, giving users the power to monitor water conditions at a glance and to manually adjust settings, such as the desired water temperature to which the system dynamically responds, recalibrating itself to meet the updated preferences, promoting high adaptability through user-friendly control.

The methodology used in the development of the SmartPool system followed the design, implementation, and evaluation of an automated system for real-time water quality management and pool safety. Figure 1 showcases the system architecture in a high-level design of the flow of information from field devices into Protocol Adapters, the Platform's core, and external applications for visualization and decision-making. The following section explains in detail the system components, data flow, and implementation details.

### A. System Architecture

The architecture of the SmartPool system follows a five-level structure, ensuring a clear division of responsibilities and functionalities. The *Perception Level* includes the physical sensors and actuators responsible for data collection and environment control. Key components include water quality sensors, which measure temperature; environmental sensors, which monitor light intensity and detect water levels; a camera, which captures real-time visual data of the pool and its surroundings; LEDs, used for signaling critical parameter levels to alert users and for enhancing overall illumination; and an alarm, which provides alerts to notify users of potential drowning incidents involving animals or children.

The *Network Level* facilitates communication between the perception level and higher levels. The system uses Wi-Fi [17] to transmit data from sensors and cameras to the Raspberry Pi [18] via the MQTT protocol [19]. As this protocol uses a publish-subscribe pattern, several topics were defined, both for the sensors and the actuators, with the strings "sensor/#" and "actuator/#", where "#" can be represented by the strings "luminosity", "distance", and "temperature" for the sensors, and "rgb/1", "rgb/2", "buzz", and "buzz/silence" for the actuators. An important consideration was a fault tolerance mechanism for Wi-Fi failures. The Arduinos [20] keep trying to establish Wi-Fi connections, publish data, and collect actionable insights.

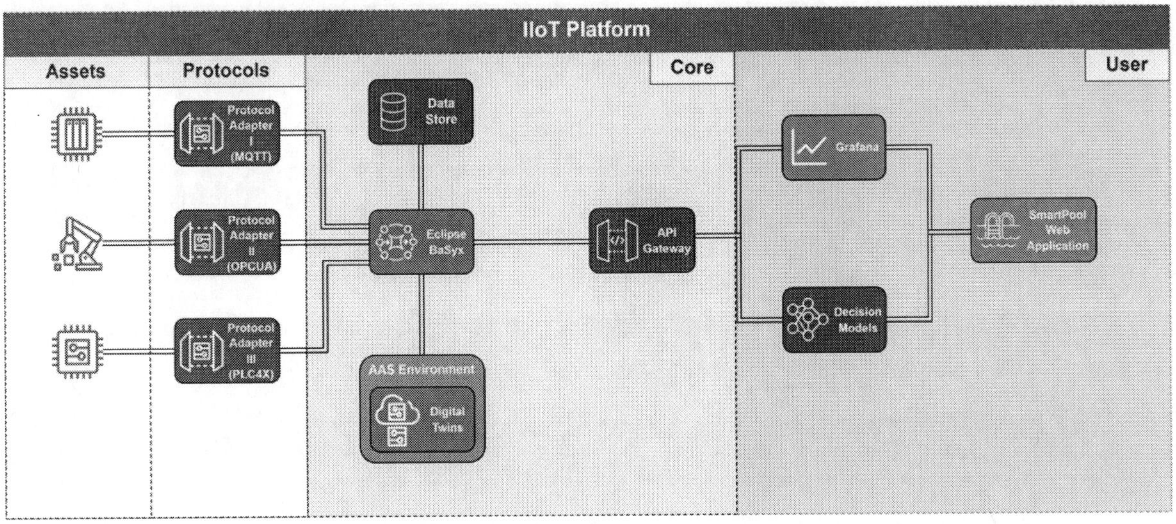


Figure 1. Architecture of the system.

Subsequently, in the *Middleware Level*, the Raspberry Pi serves as the primary central hub, handling data processing from sensors, executing decision-making algorithms, and managing communication with the AAS structure. To address potential computational power limitations, a Fog node—represented by a dedicated computer—was integrated into the architecture. The Fog node offloads some of the computational responsibilities from the Raspberry Pi, enabling the system to scale and accommodate additional central hub devices, such as those for future clients' pools. This node also hosts the AAS structure, using the open-source framework Eclipse BaSyx implementation [21]. This incorporation enables control of physical assets through their digital replicas, a standardized representation of the data, and bi-directional communication. Components of Eclipse BaSyx were deployed as Docker containers [22], ensuring efficient AAS registration and MQTT-based communication. The middleware level is responsible for storing sensor data in an InfluxDB database [23], with Telegraf [24] acting as a bridge between the MQTT broker and the database. The incorporation of Eclipse BaSyx.

*Application Level* is mainly composed by a web application providing visualizations of the collected data. As shown in Figure 2, it presents water and environment parameters, as well as the *live feed* of the pool and historical visuals created and displayed using Grafana.

Finally, the *Business Level*, which focuses on the broader operational and strategic goals of the system. This level addresses data analytics and notifications to optimize pool maintenance and enhance user safety and comfort by integrating advanced monitoring technologies.

## B. Hardware and Software Implementation

The SmartPool system incorporates a combination of hardware and software components to ensure robust functionality across all levels of the architecture. The hardware setup includes a Raspberry Pi, which acts as the primary processing and communication node, equipped with the Raspberry Pi Camera Module 2 for visual monitoring. Arduinos are utilized as intermediaries for data collection from sensors, transmitting measurements to the Raspberry Pi. Sensors and actuators are integrated to measure water quality parameters and execute corrective actions. The sensors are connected to the Arduinos, which preprocess and relay the data to the Raspberry Pi. The Raspberry Pi then processes this data and interfaces with actuators for implementing corrective measures.

The software system was developed using a combination of tools and frameworks to ensure seamless operation. An MQTT Broker was deployed on the Raspberry Pi to facilitate message processing between edge-level functionality and the AAS, enabling efficient real-time data exchange. For object detection, YOLOv8 integrated with OpenCV [25] is used to identify entities near the pool captured in the camera feed. Detection results trigger alerts and are communicated to the dashboard via the middleware. The AAS functionality is implemented using the Docker-based version of Eclipse BaSyx, which includes essential components, such as the AAS Server for hosting the digital twin representation of the pool's assets, the AAS Registry for managing and organizing multiple AAS instances, and the Databridge Component for communication with external protocols like MQTT to ensure data flow between the physical and digital twins.

A user-friendly web interface, represented in Figure 2, was developed using React [26] with Vite [27]. This interface serves as the SmartPool dashboard, providing real-time monitoring, alert notifications, and control capabilities to ensure an intuitive user experience. The interface design prioritizes a balance between usability and system capacity, as performing essential actions is equally important to overall system usability in the final product.

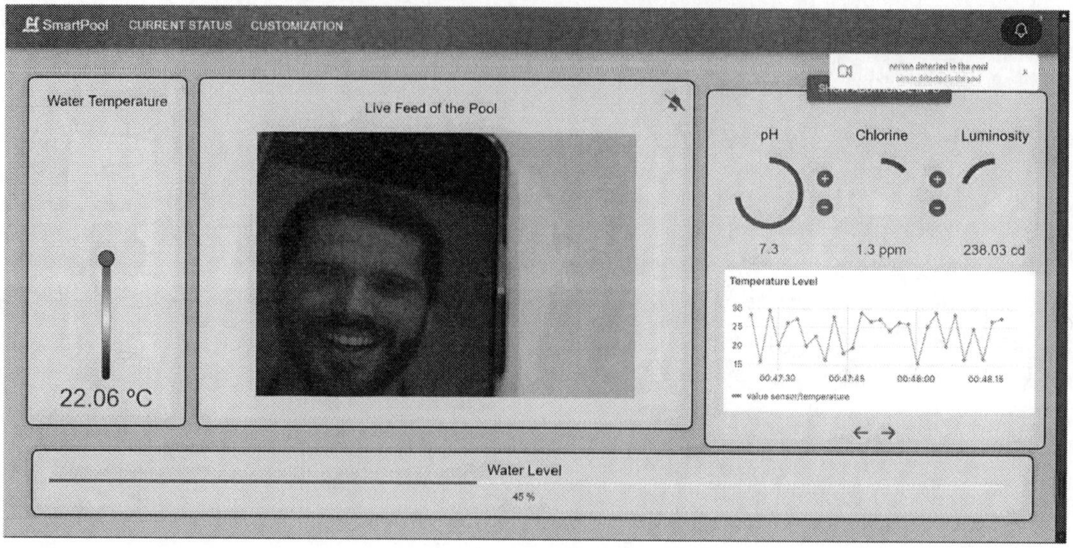


Figure 2. SmartPool UI.

## IV. Validation and Result Analysis

To comprehend the tangible impact and benefits of the SmartPool System, it is important to analyze the results in the different fields, namely: Continuous Visual Monitoring Performance; System Responsiveness; and Parameters Monitoring.

### *A. Continuous Visual Monitoring*

The system integrates intelligent recognition algorithms and real-time alert mechanisms to enhance pool safety by reducing the risk of drowning accidents. This is accomplished by a live camera feed that continuously monitors the pool and its immediate surroundings, notifying the user in the web application when any recognized entities of interest are detected (e.g., a dog near the pool). Users receive rapid alerts via the interface and can also view the live feed, ensuring they are always informed and able to respond when necessary.

A *Raspberry Pi* was used to obtain the live feed through the *Pi camera module 2*. This camera uses a Sony IMX219 8-megapixel sensor and can obtain somewhat high-definition images and video. However, due to the high strain placed on the Raspberry Pi by the various programs being run on it, the video quality and frame rate cap out at very low values. One such program is intelligent recognition, which leverages the Python library cv2 and the YoloV8 model to get the entity recognition algorithms used in the live feed. Since video capture is handled by the *Raspberry Pi*, the computationally costly frame processing, powered by the YoloV8 model, is only performed at six-second intervals. This study briefly considered offloading the object detection algorithm to a more powerful device, fully utilizing a distributed IoT architecture, but later refrained from doing so because object detection should be independent of device connectivity and achieve low latency for critical and urgent situations, such as when a child or a pet falls into the water. The final implemented setup optimizes performance and energy consumption by reducing the image processing frequency while still ensuring timely detection of any noteworthy events.

This study utilizes the Raspberry Pi as the central processing unit within the pool environment. Video frames captured by the Pi camera are transmitted as file properties of an AAS via POST requests. These files can then be retrieved and processed at the application level, enabling the delivery of high-quality images to the front end and providing a live feed of the pool.

The real-time visual monitoring system demonstrated strong capabilities in detecting and identifying entities near the pool, such as animals or people. Using the YOLOv8 model integrated with the Raspberry Pi, in a testing phase, the system, after performing the entity recognition process, was able to send alerts with less than a second delay every time with light or partial obstruction having little to no effect on the result.

To ensure near-certainty in the entity recognition, the confidence threshold defined was 0.7, meaning that the user would only receive an entity recognition notification if the model was 70% certain of its decision. Although the camera quality was high, with video live streams maintaining a stable resolution of 1080p, due to computational strain on the Raspberry Pi, the entity recognition was only performed once every 6 seconds.

### *B. System Responsiveness*

During testing, the web-based User Interface (UI), represented in Figure 2, consistently displayed updated pool conditions with delays of less than 5 seconds. System notifications, including alert information and corresponding alarm sounds, were delivered within 1 second of completing the Event Response Process, even under both normal and high-stress environments. The dashboard demonstrated seamless responsiveness on both mobile and desktop platforms, maintaining its functionality and design integrity across devices.

User-triggered actions, such as toggling lights or muting/unmuting alarms, were executed within 2 to 3 seconds under normal conditions. In hardware-stressed scenarios, delays increased slightly, ranging between 6 and 7 seconds.

### C. Parameters Monitoring

The system, represented in Figure 3, effectively monitored critical water quality parameters, including temperature, light intensity, and water level, with updated values consistently displayed on the interface. Readings were recorded with minimal delays and achieved near-real-time accuracy, providing reliable data on pool conditions.

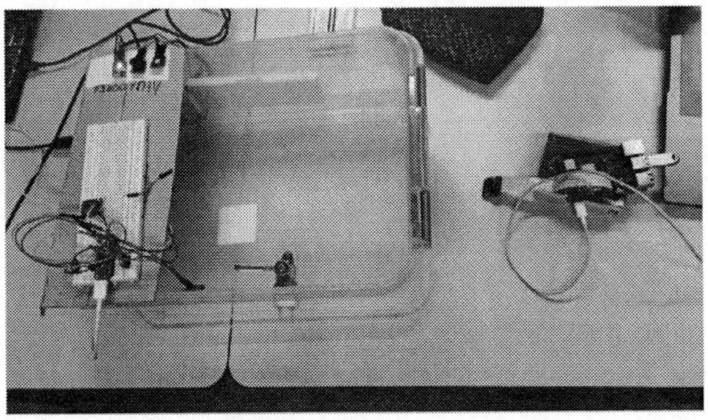

Figure 3. SmartPool Prototype.

The water level monitoring, while generally satisfactory, experienced occasional inaccuracies due to the transparent nature of water affecting the distance sensor. However, these discrepancies were minimized after stabilization.

All actuators within the system performed as expected during testing, ensuring the successful execution of automated responses and user-triggered actions.

## V. Discussion

Having successfully achieved its primary objectives as a prototype, the SmartPool system shows significant promise in automating pool maintenance and improving safety. Real-time visual monitoring with YOLOv8 delivered accurate alerts despite the hardware limitations caused by Raspberry Pi's processing constraints, which led to some slightly longer response times. Improved hardware or more efficient detection models specific to such devices could address this issue. The system's sustainability can also be improved by integrating energy-efficient components or renewable energies. In outdoor pool areas, solar power could be a viable eco-friendly energy source. However, an increase in energy usage may be the result of a compromise to increase the system responsiveness and the safety of the users of the pool.

Water quality monitoring for temperature and light intensity was effective, although the water level sensor showed occasional inaccuracies. Sensor calibration or even alternative technologies could help tackle this problem.

Another feature lacking in this implementation is security. MQTT protocol and POST requests to transmit information between the various physical assets of the pool to the middleware. These packets, however, are not encrypted and do not have any integrity checks. An attacker can not only see the private information in the packets, including sensor information and the images captured by the camera, but they can also change the packets at will. The attacker can change parameters meant for the actuators during transmission, which can cause unwanted behaviors. Another problem is that the nodes used in the system are not authenticated, and that leaves room for spoofing attacks, where an attacker can trick the nodes and middleware into sending the data to them instead of the actual nodes and components. Even though these issues present a big concern to a normal system, this study does not address them, as this implementation serves as a prototype not meant to be fully deployable, as is, in the real world.

While user feedback was positive regarding the dashboard's intuitive and functional design, some improvements have been suggested. The interface is simple, and while it works adequately in its current state, enhancements to customization could be made to better support more complex systems.

## VI. Conclusion & Future Work

The SmartPool system demonstrates how sensors, actuators, and data-driven strategies can enhance pool maintenance, safety, and user experience. By automating the monitoring and adjustment of critical water quality parameters, the system reduces manual intervention while improving safety, operational efficiency, and sustainability. Real-time visual surveillance, powered by advanced recognition algorithms, further enhances safety by detecting and responding to potential risks, such as a child falling into the pool.

Even though the prototype shows that automated pool administration is feasible, there are still a number of areas that might be improved:

- Advanced Machine Learning: Incorporating more sophisticated machine learning models could improve decision-making and anomaly detection. Enhanced hardware performance would support faster processing and more frequent data transmission, reducing the current three-second interval and enabling more comprehensive real-time monitoring.
- Improved Security: Strengthening system security is a critical priority. Future implementations will include a Certificate Authority to issue certificates for Fog nodes and middleware components, enabling robust identification and authentication. By employing Transport Layer Security (TLS) on top of the MQTT protocol, all transmissions will be encrypted and safeguarded against tampering. These measures aim to resolve the security vulnerabilities present in the current system.
- Sustainability Enhancements: The system's environmental footprint can be minimized by adopting energy-efficient hardware and integrating renewable energy sources, such as solar panels, to power its components.
- Scalability: Expanding the platform's scalability will enable it to support larger facilities or more complex aquatic environments, broadening its applicability.

This research highlights the transformative potential of IoT and CPS in pool management, showcasing innovations that promote convenience, safety, and environmental responsibility. By addressing the identified limitations—such as enhancing machine learning capabilities, improving security, and ensuring sustainability—future developments can cater to the diverse needs of pool operators and users, paving the way for smarter, more sustainable aquatic solutions.

## Acknowledgment

This work is financially supported by national funds through the FCT/MCTES (PIDDAC), under the Associate Laboratory Advanced Production and Intelligent Systems – ARISE LA/P/0112/2020 (DOI 10.54499/LA/P/0112/2020) and the Base Funding (UIDB/00147/2020) and Programmatic Funding (UIDP/00147/2020) of the R&D Unit Center for Systems and Technologies – SYSTEC.

## References

[1] A. Jemat, S. Yussof, S. S. Sameon, and N. A. Alya Rosnizam, "IoT-Based System for Real-Time Swimming Pool Water Quality Monitoring," *Lecture Notes in Computer Science (including subseries Lecture Notes in Artificial Intelligence and Lecture Notes in Bioinformatics)*, vol. 13051 LNCS, pp. 332–341, 2021, Cited by: 3. DOI: 10.1007/978-3-030-90235-3_29.

[2] A. Angdresey, L. Sitanayah, and V. J. A. Sampul, "Monitoring and Predicting Water Quality in Swimming Pools," *EPI International Journal of Engineering*, vol. 8, no. 2, pp. 119–125, 2020, Accessed from https://doi.org/10.25042/epi-ije.082020.05. DOI: 10.25042/epi-ije.082020.05.

[3] S. Zeb *et al.*, "Industrial digital twins at the nexus of NextG wireless networks and computational intelligence: A survey," *Journal of Network and Computer Applications*, vol. 200, p. 103 309, 2022, ISSN: 1084-8045. DOI: https://doi.org/10.1016/j.jnca.2021.103309.

[4] M. Kaur, V. Mishra, and P. Maheshwari, "The Convergence of Digital Twin, IoT, and Machine Learning: Transforming Data into Action," in *Internet of Things*, Springer, Cham, 2020, pp. 3–17. DOI: 10.1007/978-3-030-18732-3_1.

[5] A. Redelinghuys, A. Basson, and K. Kruger, "A six-layer architecture for the digital twin: a manufacturing case study implementation," *Journal of Intelligent Manufacturing*, vol. 31, no. 6, pp. 1383–1402, 2020. DOI: 10.1007/s10845-019-01516-6.

[6] S. A. Hamid *et al.*, "IoT based Water Quality Monitoring System and Evaluation," in *2020 10th IEEE International Conference on Control System, Computing and Engineering (ICCSCE)*, 2020, pp. 102–106. DOI: 10.1109/ICCSCE50387.2020.9204931.

[7] V. Lakshmikantha *et al.*, "IoT based smart water quality monitoring system," *Global Transitions Proceedings*, vol. 2, no. 2, pp. 181–186, 2021, International Conference on Computing System and its Applications (ICCSA- 2021), ISSN: 2666-285X. DOI: https://doi.org/10.1016/j.gltp.2021.08.062.

[8] A. Sangeetha *et al.*, "Smart Swimming Pool Management System (SSPMS) using IoT," in *2023 International Conference on Innovative Data Communication Technologies and Application (ICIDCA)*, 2023, pp. 840–846. DOI: 10.1109/ICIDCA56705.2023.10099729.

[9] K. J. S. Raj *et al.*, "Enhancing Pool Safety and Efficiency with an IoT Supported Monitoring System," in *2023 3rd International Conference on Pervasive Computing and Social Networking (ICPCSN)*, 2023, pp. 1232–1237. DOI: 10.1109/ICPCSN58827.2023.00208.

[10] J. P. Christopher, S. D. Damayanti, and M. Suryanegara, "Investigating IoT-LoRa Technology for The Underwater System Application," in *2023 IEEE 8th International Conference on Recent Advances and Innovations in Engineering (ICRAIE)*, 2023, pp. 1–4. DOI: 10.1109/ICRAIE59459.2023.10468069.

[11] A. Glória, F. Cercas, and N. Souto, "Design and implementation of an IoT gateway to create smart environments," *Procedia Computer Science*, vol. 109, pp. 568–575, 2017, 8th International Conference on Ambient Systems, Networks and Technologies, ANT-2017 and the 7th International Conference on Sustainable Energy Information Technology, SEIT 2017, 16-19 May 2017, Madeira, Portugal, ISSN: 1877-0509. DOI: https://doi.org/10.1016/j.procs.2017.05.343.

[12] M. Elgorma *et al.*, "A review of methods for detecting and preventing drowning incorporating various techniques, devices and technologies," in *2nd International Conference on Electrical Engineering and Automatic Control*, 2024, pp. 1–6.

[13] S. Karthik, D. Priya E.L., G. Anand K.R., and A. Sharmila, "IoT Based Safety Enhanced Swimming Pool with Embedded Techniques to reduce drowning accidents," in *2020 International Conference on Smart Electronics and Communication (ICOSEC)*, 2020, pp. 843–847. DOI: 10.1109/ICOSEC49089.2020.9215247.

[14] N. Chilwant and M. S. Kulkarni, "Open Asset Administration Shell for Industrial Systems," *Manufacturing Letters*, vol. 20, pp. 15–21, 2019, ISSN: 2213-8463. DOI: https://doi.org/10.1016/j.mfglet.2019.02.002.

[15] B. Chen *et al.*, "Edge Computing in IoT-Based Manufacturing," *IEEE Communications Magazine*, vol. 56, pp. 103–109, 2018. DOI: 10.1109/MCOM.2018.1701231.

[16] F. Haouari, R. Faraj, and J. Jaam, "Fog Computing Potentials, Applications, and Challenges," *2018 International Conference on Computer and Applications (ICCA)*, pp. 399–406, 2018. DOI: 10.1109/COMAPP.2018.8460182.

[17] S. S. Salwe and K. K. Naik, "Heterogeneous Wireless Network for IoT Applications," *IETE Technical Review*, vol. 36, pp. 61–68, 2019. DOI: 10.1080/02564602.2017.1400412.

[18] E. Upton and G. Halfacree, *Raspberry Pi User Guide*, 3rd. Indianapolis, IN, USA: Wiley, 2014, ISBN: 978-1118921661.

[19] A. Banks and R. Gupta, "MQTT Version 3.1.1," 2014, [Online]. Available: https://docs.oasis-open.org/mqtt/mqtt/v3.1.1/mqtt-v3.1.1.html (visited on 02/11/2025).

[20] M. Banzi and M. Shiloh, *Getting Started with Arduino*, 3rd. Sebastopol, CA, USA: Maker Media, Inc., 2014, ISBN: 978-1449363338.

[21] E. Foundation, "Eclipse BaSyx Documentation," 2023, [Online]. Available: https://www.eclipse.org/basyx/ (visited on 02/11/2025).

[22] I. Docker, "Docker Documentation," 2023, [Online]. Available: https://docs.docker.com/ (visited on 02/11/2025).

[23] InfluxData, "InfluxDB Documentation," 2025, [Online]. Available: https://docs.influxdata.com/influxdb/ (visited on 02/11/2025).

[24] InfluxData, "Telegraf Documentation," 2025, [Online]. Available: https://docs.influxdata.com/telegraf/ (visited on 02/11/2025).

[25] OpenCV Team, "OpenCV: Open Source Computer Vision Library," 2025, [Online]. Available: https://opencv.org/ (visited on 02/11/2025).

[26] Meta Platforms, Inc., "React: A JavaScript Library for Building User Interfaces," 2025, [Online]. Available: https://reactjs.org/ (visited on 02/11/2025).

[27] Evan You and Vite Contributors, "Vite: Next Generation Frontend Tooling," 2025, [Online]. Available: https://vitejs.dev/ (visited on 02/11/2025).

# Situated Learners in a Sequential Decision-Making Setting

Timur Kasimov*
*Computer Science (Grinnell College)*
Grinnell, USA
email: kasimovt@grinnell.edu

Shinon Takei*
*Computer Science (Grinnell College)*
Grinnell, USA
email: takeishi@grinnell.edu

Hanfeng Lu
*Computer Science (Grinnell College)*
Grinnell, USA
email: hlu002327@gmail.com

Mingi Lee
*Computer Science (Grinnell College)*
Grinnell, USA
email: leemingi@grinnell.edu

Fernanda Eliott
*Computer Science (Grinnell College)*
Grinnell, USA
email: eliottfe@grinnell.edu

***Abstract*—Tricky coordination challenges can emerge from combining distributed settings with independent learners (since these learners have only access to limited information). Still, treating agents as independent learners can help mitigate the problem of observing multiple agents' joint actions. Here, we detail and examine the Discrete Smart Surface benchmark with two goals: 1. Follow a call to the Multi-Agent Systems community to consider the environment as an important entity at the application level, and 2. Show/discuss our experimental results for combining independent learners with the Discrete Smart Surface benchmark under various dimensions and agent-weighting systems. Investigating challenges in Multi-Agent Systems can be particularly insightful for applications that rely on multiple decision-makers; thus, we thoroughly reflect on our experimental results and exemplify challenges, such as action shadowing.**

***Keywords-action shadowing; discrete actuator arrays; independent learners; sequential decision making.***

## I. Introduction

Given the accelerated advances in computational infrastructure over the past few years, is it still advantageous to study Multi-Agent Systems (MAS) in tabular settings? Or, in other words, what can we gain from investigating tabular worlds? As Gronauer and Diepold [1] overview the landscape of the multiagent deep reinforcement learning literature, they help us answer that question: tabular worlds still offer insights to investigating crucial challenges in MAS – "simple worlds remain a fertile ground for further research, especially for problems like shadowed equilibria, non-stationarity or alter-exploration problems and continue to matter for modern deep learning approaches" [1].

In fact, Matignon, Laurent, and Le Fort-Piat [2] investigate coordination challenges in MAS; more specifically, challenges that independent learners (see Section II) must overcome to learn and accomplish coordination tasks. Inspired by a distributed manipulation and discrete actuator arrays [3] (see Section II), the authors provide the *Discrete Smart Surface* benchmark, which we call by DSSb. The benchmark enlightens the investigation of challenges faced by applications that rely on multiple decision-makers influencing each other's decisions, such as in multi-robot control.

A fixed 2D grid of actuators defines the DSSb, and its successful accomplishment requires the coordination between many situated agents to move an object to a goal location (see our toy example in Figure 1, which is detailed in Section III). With the benchmark, the authors [2] sought to investigate many agents coordinating actions in a Markov Game [4] (they used a $9 \times 30$ grid of 270 actuators). A trial starts with an object at the initial location (grid's top-center as a default) and ends when the object reaches the terminal state (grid's bottom-center as a default).

We build on their work [2] to detail the DSSb and experimentally test it under various settings. *But why pick the DSSb instead of another benchmark, such as the popular pursuit domain [5]?* We are particularly interested in the DSSb due to its focus on situated agents: it enables us to run many *situated* agents in a task that requires coordination between them. Moreover, situated agents help to highlight, within the MAS literature, the importance of having the environment as a first-order abstraction [6]. Hence, the DSSb not only helps to investigate challenges in MAS but also illustrates the importance of distinguishing between agent and environment – such importance motivated us to detail the DSSb, which is one of our contributions.

Focusing on challenges in MAS, an interesting question to ask is: in what ways can the DSSb help us visualize and get a better understanding of action shadowing? We sought to answer that question as we contextualize and explain our experimental results. In particular, we investigated questions such as:

- How does the agents' success in coordinating actions change as we increase the grid dimensions?
- How do the action pairings change as the agents learn to coordinate actions?
- How do the agents' weights in the decision process of moving the object impact the task's success? And does an agent's location determine its role (or importance) in a task's success?
- What is the role of the penalty areas, and how does that affect the learning opportunities of an agent situated in a penalty area? Thus, regarding *learning the task*, can we say that agents are "luckier" according to their location

in the grid? Or, in other words, does an agent's location determine its learning process/opportunities?
- What does action shadowing look like in the DSSb?

We investigate these questions in Sections III and IV; and our contributions are to:

1) Detail the DSSb while making a clear distinction between agent and environment – following a call from [6], and in the hope that others will reflect on the importance of such a distinction, especially today, with AI systems merging deeply into our realities and the physical/digital boundaries getting blurrier.
2) Show and discuss our experimental results for combining independent learners with the DSSb under various dimensions and agent-weighting systems.

In future work, we will expand our experiments to cover more agent dimensions and weighting systems; we will analyze and contrast them with other settings, such as the pursuit domain [5], the Michigan Intelligent Coordination Experiment (MICE) [7], multi-turn games [8] and other settings, such as [9] and [10].

This work is organized as follows: we introduce our work in Section I, provide background information and related literature in Section II, detail the functioning of the DSSb in Section III, provide observations to support experimental analysis followed by experimental results in Section IV, and conclude in Section V. Finally, the questions provided in the Introduction (Section I) are addressed in Sections III - IV.

## II. Background and Related Work

In this section, we provide background information as we visit related literature and contextualize the DSSb, which addresses situated agents, independent learners, identical payoffs, and Markov games. We start by describing the work [3] that inspired the design of DSSb [2].

**Distributed Manipulation and Discrete Actuator Arrays.** Luntz and Messner [3] build upon their previous model [11] to create a distributed manipulation system that coordinates to induce motion and manipulate larger objects. The authors explore distributed control after considering it would be impractical for a single centralized controller to control thousands of cells. Their system uses actuator arrays of many small stationary elements called cells. If one wished to visualize the system in the context of a macro-scale actuator, one could do it through a fixed 2D grid of motorized wheels. For intuitive purposes, here is a loose example to mentally picture the system: imagine a 2D grid of motorized wheels moving checked bags at an airport. An object lies on supporting cells, and as the object moves, its supporting cells change. Cells that support the object provide a traction force, and their combined action, through coordination, determines the object's motion (*both* translation and rotation). The modeling considers a) the interaction between actuators and the object, b) the object's weight distribution among the support, and c) the system's discrete nature. In the system, each cell communicates with its neighboring cells, and each cell is equipped with binary sensors to detect the presence of an object [3].

**Situated Agents.** A situated agent has spatial coordinates and interacts with other agents in a hosting environment [12]. In response to a bottleneck, [12] propose an approach to the modeling and simulation of large-scale situated MAS. The observed bottleneck sits within parallel/distributed simulation of situated agents such that the environment represents a substantial shared variable that requires cautious treatment, and regular agent access to environment information can quickly become a bottleneck that diminishes system performance and scalability.

**MAS and Environments.** Weyns, Vizzari and Holvoet [6] identify issues among the MAS community in defining environments, e.g., "environment" may refer to a) the logical entity in which agents and resources are embedded, or b) the software infrastructure on which it is executed, or even c) the running underlying hardware infrastructure. They illustrate those issues through a situated setting (like the DSSb, in which agents have an explicit position in the environment), as they propose a three-layer model to help distinguish between the environment and the infrastructure on which the MAS is deployed. According to the authors, although there are aspects conceptually apart from the agents themselves and thus should not be assigned or hosted inside agents, the MAS community often considers the environment as infrastructure instead of an important entity at the application level.

Weyns and colleagues [13] aim to push the community to make the environment's logical functionalities explicit, or in other words, to treat concerns of environments as first-class entities. While describing the MAS application layer, the authors identify two classes of concerns: the ones related to the structure of the environment and the ones related to the environment's activity. "Agents and objects of a MAS share a common environment. The agents as well as the objects are dynamically interrelated to each other. It is the role of the environment to define the rules under which these relationships can exist and can evolve. As such the environment acts as a structuring entity for the MAS" [13]. We follow the authors' call as we make a clear distinction between agent and environment in the DSSb, in addition to treating concerns of environments as first-class entities (see Section III).

**Agent Coordination.** Malone and Crowston [14] provide a definition useful for highlighting aspects of a task that requires coordination: it is "the act of managing interdependencies between activities performed to achieve a goal". Building on that, "agent coordination is the ability to manage the interdependencies of activities between agents while agent cooperation is the process used for an agent to voluntarily enter a relationship with another to achieve a system derived goal" [15].

Tan [16] compares independent learners with cooperative agents (defining *cooperation* in the sense of agents sharing episodes, learned policies, or instantaneous information). Sukhbaatar, Szlam, and Fergus [8] apply fully cooperative tasks to examine CommNet, a neural model that uses continuous communication; the model uses multiple agents that learn to communicate alongside their policy. According to the

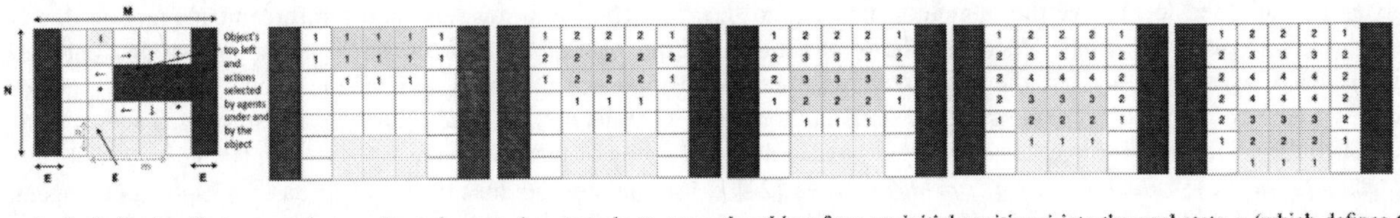

Figure 1. **Left.** Each cell corresponds to a situated agent. Agents task: to move the object from an initial position $i$ into the goal state $g$ (which defines the terminal state). The $3 \times 2$ object is color-coded in blue. Arrows inside the grid correspond to actions selected by agents under or by the object (circles for 'stay still'). The leftmost and rightmost columns are penalty areas, which agents also occupy.

authors, their findings show simple but effective strategies for solving the tasks since, in some of the experiments, it is possible to interpret the language used by the agents. Although the DSSb applies non-communicative agents, the work described in [8] is worth mentioning due to one of the tested environments, which is a $14 \times 14$ grid. It consists of a 4-way junction: at each time step, a new car enters the grid with a certain probability from each of the four directions; each car occupies a single cell and is randomly assigned to one of three possible routes.

Switching gears to a robot's manipulative repertoire, Stuber and colleagues [17] describe pushing as an essential motion primitive and that, despite a considerable amount of work and models on robot pushing, there would be work to be done on generalizations to novel objects – emphasizing the non-triviality of the problem. For instance, robotic grasping and manipulation would not be trivial even if we considered ideal conditions (described by the authors as structured environments in which an agent has access to a complete model of the environment and ideal sensing abilities). The authors mention the importance of using MAS to move large-scale objects in real-world applications and how control and decision-making are critical issues in those scenarios. For instance, agents must not only coordinate actions, but the point of view changes as a consequence of their actions, bringing yet another challenge: to predict outcomes from pushing given by the action of multiple agents. Finally, Acuña and Schrater [18] provide an interesting study on human decision-making and structure learning in sequential decision tasks.

**Coordination and Communication Issues in Robotic Applications.** Matignon, Jeanpierre, and Mouaddib [19] study multi-robot exploration under communication breaks constraints. Working under the assumptions of full local observability, limited information sharing between the agents, and breaks in communication, their research addresses global and local coordination of decentralized decision-makers. They develop and apply a method to multi-robot exploration scenarios; according to the authors, experimental results in real-world contexts show that their method is robust to communication breaks and successfully helps to coordinate a team of robots.

**Independent Learners and Markov Games.** In Robotic tasks that require many agents to coordinate actions to accomplish a task, it is tricky to observe the agents' joint actions [2] (e.g., find and coordinate actions to collect and move an object). To navigate the issue, we can treat the agents as independent (non-communicative) learning agents [20]. In opposition to joint-action learners, independent learners are agents that ignore or cannot observe the actions and reinforcements of other agents in the environment and, therefore, can apply the off-policy temporal difference control algorithm [21] Q-learning [22] in a classic sense and dismiss other agents' existance [20]. However, in the case of distributed settings, the limited information brings about interesting challenges, or "pathologies" [1] for independent learners (which we explore in Section IV).

Boutilier [23] provides an insightful bridge analogy to think of coordination problems when agents have common interests. Consider a team of agents modeled as acting on behalf of a single individual and, therefore, acting to maximize the individual's utility. Suppose a team needs to cross a bridge that can only support one agent at a time; in that case, agents would need to coordinate the ordering of crossing to avoid the bridge collapsing (and destroying the crossing agents along with it). For each agent, the crossing ordering may not be important as long as it crosses it and pursues its goals. Further, Boutilier [23] reflects on scenarios where each agent's abilities are such that it does not really matter what agent pursues which goal (as long as all or most of the goals are pursued). When there is some flexibility in each agent's role, they may end up pursuing the same goal, and lack of coordination can range from delays in accomplishing a task to never really accomplishing it. Such context can be generalized to other team contexts, such as logistics planning [23].

Within robotics applications, Matignon and colleagues [2] are interested in those in which a group of robots can accomplish a task faster than a single robot. The authors, similarly to [23], adopt the terminologies *cooperative robots* and *learning algorithms in fully cooperative MAS* to convey settings in which agents share common interests or the same utility function, *i.e.,* there is a correspondence between each agent's achievement and the group's and therefore, the learning goal is defined as maximizing the common discounted return.

Or, as [23] puts it, fully cooperative MAS in which we assume that it is possible to set a common coordination mechanism and that agents do not have a reason to deliberate strategically. The authors [2] use *Markov Games* instead of *Stochastic Games* to distinguish their settings from *stochastic (non-deterministic) Markov Games*. "Markov games are a superset of Markov decision processes and matrix games, including both multiple agents and multiple states", and all agents are supposed to observe the complete state $s$, and the transition and reward functions depend on the joint action of agents [2]. If all agents are fed the same rewards, then the Markov game is called *fully cooperative* by some authors, as "a best-interest action of one agent is also a best-interest action of every agent" [2] – *identical payoff stochastic game* [24] is another possible terminology. We describe the DSSb next.

## III. The Discrete Smart Surface Benchmark

In this section, we detail a DSSb environment and the rules that dynamically connect agents and objects. In Figure 1, we illustrate the DSSb: suppose the agents coordinate their actions to move the object to the goal state using the optimum number of steps. Then, **from left to right**, the five images show the object's position step by step within a trial, whereas numbers progressively show how often under/by agents played a role as they moved the object to the goal state. The object reaches the terminal state in the final step, which is not shown here.

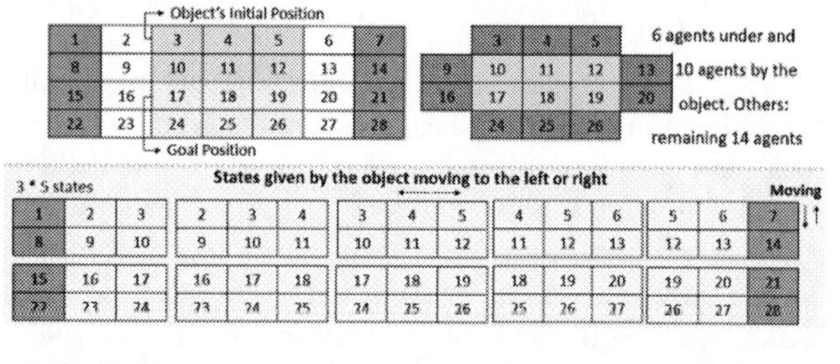


Figure 2. Upper left: a toy example; numbers within cells represent a situated agent. Upper right: a state in which 16 agents' actions play a role in the transition function $F$; remaining 14 agents are ignored ($w_s = 0$). Lower level: 15 possible states given by the grid and the object's dimensions (intermediary row omitted).

In the DSSb, agents have common interests, and a common coordination mechanism is assumed; the agents' task is to identify a joint sequence of actions that maximize the long-term common discounted return. Let a Discrete Smart Surface $G = \{M, N, E, m, n, S, F, R, A, L\}$, where (see Figure 1 left):

1) $M$ is the width, and $N$ the height of a 2D array of actuators, each driven by an agent. Therefore, there are $M \times N$ actuators – we refer to each actuator as an *agent*.

2) A motion of a 2D object that is placed on the 2D grid's surface is determined by a weighted sum of the agents' actions. The object does not rotate and cannot leave the surface.

3) $m$ is the width, and $n$ is the height of the object ($m < M$ and $n < N$).

4) $E$ is the width of the grid's right and left borders, which are penalty areas. Borders have equal width and height, such as $1 \times N$ each.

5) $S$ is the set of states. Each possible object's position defines a unique state; hence, there are $(M-m+1)(N-n+1)$ states. Initial and terminal states correspond to the object's initial and goal positions (we interchangeably use terminal/goal state).

6) Trials start from placing the object on the initial position $i$ and finish once the object's top left reaches the goal state $g$.

7) The state transition and reinforcement function depend on the agents' joint actions. $F$ is the transition function that applies a weighted sum of the agents' actions to decide the object's motion/state transition. $F$ categorizes agents into three groups: agents by the object, agents under the object, and remaining agents. Each group has a weight that impacts the transition dynamics: $w_b, w_u, w_s$, respectively.

8) $R$ is the reinforcement function: agents receive identical payoffs.

9) $A$ is the set of actions available to each agent, and $A = \{\text{left, right, up, down, still}\}$. At each time step, agents select an action from $A$ and simultaneously execute it.

• Finally, $L$ represents the agent structure applied to drive the actuators, such as the agents' implemented reinforcement learning techniques and action-selection mechanism. Although the agents act in an environment that offers affordances [25], [26], agents are distinct from the environment. Thus, within $G$, we group two classes of concerns: the ones related to the environment's structure and the ones related to its activity.

To conclude, a developer should keep in mind that there are parameters intrinsic to $F$, $R$, and $L$ (e.g., weight values, reinforcement values, and learning rates); also, if one wishes to introduce uncertainty to account for actuator errors (e.g., actuators or sensors presenting issues due to unexpected external or internal factors), that can be done by making an agent apply a random action with a small probability [2].

### A. Sequential Decision-Making and Trials

In the DSSb, a simulation is a defined number of trials run in sequence, and agents must learn to coordinate actions to move the object to the terminal/goal state. A trial starts with the object at the initial state (even if random) and ends once it reaches the terminal state. A trial lasts for at least the minimum number of steps needed to successfully accomplish the task (object reaching the goal state). Within a trial:

- Agents have access to their own actions and current state (given by the object's top-left position) but *not* to other agents' actions. Agents simultaneously select an action.
- The transition function $F$ uses the agents' actions and corresponding weights $w_b, w_u, w_s$ (which are dynamically matched given an agent's location in relation to the object's position) to set the next state (object's motion).
- The state transition triggers the reinforcement function, which feeds identical payoffs to all agents.
- Agents use their learning mechanisms to learn and select actions in response to the environment.
- A trial ends once the object reaches the goal state (or if the trial meets another pre-defined halt condition corresponding to a task's failure, such as hitting a maximum number of steps).

**Does an agent's location interfere with the number of times it will participate in the object's motion?** Yes; in fact, given the initial and goal states and weights $w_b, w_u, w_s$, we can dissect how often an agent's actions are to be considered by the transition function $F$. Observe Figure 1 left and note that five steps are needed for the object ($3 \times 2$ size and color-coded in blue) to reach the goal state. Now, suppose a) an enough number of agents have learned to move the object from the initial state $i$ to the goal state $g$ (both color-coded in yellow), and b) only agents under or by the object matter, in other words, $w_u > 0$, $w_b > 0$, and $w_s = 0$. **The sequential images in Figure 1 show, step by step within a trial, how many times each agent's action plays a role in the state transition (we omit zeros for clarity).**

Therefore, agents' actions and corresponding locations in the grid are key to contextualizing experimental results for the DSSb. We reflect on that and bridge it to challenges in MAS. Does that mean that an agent's location interferes with its role (or importance) in the task? To answer that question, we built another toy example, shown in Figure 2, upper left.

Consider settings as follows: $M = 7$ and $N = 4$, $m = 3$ and $n = 2$. Therefore, there are 15 possible states, shown in Figure 2, lower part (we omit the third-row states for space reasons). These are the states that follow as the object moves: five columns sideways by three rows in the up/down directions. Within the states, we show the corresponding agents that would be under the object. At each time step, the object's top-left provides $s^t$, the state $s$ at the time step $t$. As in the other toy example, we consider $w_b > 0$, $w_u > 0$, and $w_s = 0$. Finally, Figure 2 upper right depicts a state with the following agents under the object: 10-12 and 17-19. Now, see the interplay between state and agent role/importance: in this state, only 16 out of 28 agents play a role (agents by and under the object only). Hence, Figure 2 helps notice that the number of agents by the object varies as the object moves: for this example, 5 agents if at the corners, 7 if at the top or bottom states, 8 sideways, and 10 otherwise – whereas the number of agents under the object remains constant.

## IV. Experiments

In this section, we experimentally investigate situated independent learners in a sequential decision-making setting as defined by the DSSb. We test five different grid dimensions: $\{7 \times 7;\ 9 \times 9;\ 11 \times 11;\ 13 \times 13;\ 15 \times 15\}$; therefore, the resulting number of tested agents is, respectively: 49, 81, 121, 169, 225. For clarity, we refer to the "situated independent learners" simply as "agents".

In addition, we ran five weighting settings per grid dimension. To accomplish that, we set different weights for agents by and under the object; the weights are: $\{w_b = 1,\ w_u = 1\}$; and $\{w_b = 1,\ w_u = 5\}$; and $\{w_b = 3,\ w_u = 5\}$; and $\{w_b = 5,\ w_u = 1\}$; and $\{w_b = 5,\ w_u = 3\}$. The higher the weight, the higher the impact of an agent category on deciding the transition dynamics given by $F$ (i.e., on deciding the object's motion/state transition). Note that we kept $w_s = 0$ consistent across all experiments. Other parameters and settings kept consistent across experiments are:

1) A simulation consists of multiple trials run in sequence (simulations are independent of each other).
2) A trial begins with the object at the initial state (grid's top-center) and terminates once the agents manage to move it to the terminal state (grid's bottom-center). Therefore, one can use $N - n$ to obtain the minimum number of steps required to complete a trial.
3) Object size $m = 3$ and $n = 2$.
4) Anytime the object moves to the left or right from the initial state, it enters the penalty area $E$. To completely avoid a penalty area, the object must remain in the exact middle of the grid throughout an entire trial. If the object remains in the penalty area, it triggers a negative reinforcement at every step it stays there.
5) If multiple actions have the same weighted sum of agents' actions, $F$ chooses randomly among those.
6) As a result of a state transition, all agents receive reinforcement $r = N$ if the object reaches the goal state; a punishment $r = -0.5$ if the object is on a penalty area, and $r = -0.1$ otherwise.
7) Learning phase *vs.* performance phase: we alternate the learning and performance phases such that every *odd* trial is a learning phase whereas every *even* trial is a performance phase. In the latter, there is no learning and agents pick their current best response (randomly between them, if more than one action).
8) Our results depict the performance phase, and they are averaged across 100 simulations for the *performance* phase only.
9) We used the Java programming language (Java 17, more specifically), and followed the practices from [27].

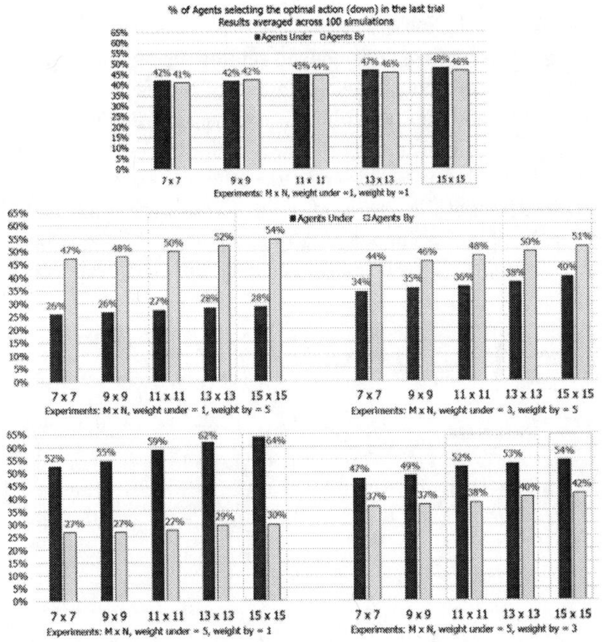


Figure 3. Results for the last trial only: distribution of "down" actions *per* agent category and across experiments. Results averaged across 100 simulations.

**Total number of trials.** To facilitate the data graphics visualization, we ran a different number of trials per grid dimension (the larger the grid, the higher the number of trials within a simulation).

**Agent Structure.** The applied reinforcement learning techniques and related parameters are kept consistent across experiments and are as follows: each agent implements the Q-Learning algorithm [22], [28] with the $\epsilon$-greedy policy with a fixed exploration rate of $10\%$ and a discount rate $\gamma = 0.9$ so that the return objective takes future rewards more strongly [21]. For the learning rate, we use $\alpha = 1/k$, where $k$ is the number of times the state-action pair $(s, a)$ has occurred so far.

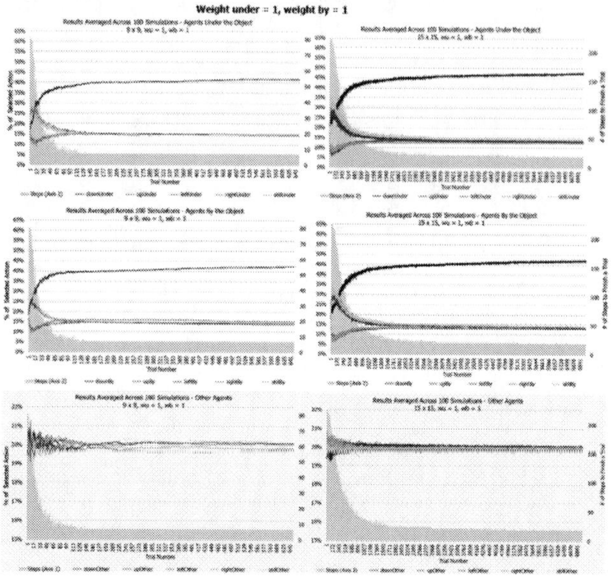


Figure 4. Weights: $w_u = 1$, $w_b = 1$, $w_s = 0$. Over trials, the distribution of actions' percentage *per* agent category, and the number of steps taken to complete a trial. Left: $9 \times 9$ grid. Right: $15 \times 15$ grid. Results averaged across 100 simulations.

**Observations to Support Experimental Analysis:**

1) The number of agents under the object is consistent over trials since the object's shape does not change.
2) However, the number of agents by the object varies according to the object's position; see Figure 2. The object's motion implies that the group of agents under and by the object changes over time.
3) Therefore, an agent may participate in the three categories within the same trial: under, by, and remaining. However, once central agents learn to select the down action, agents away from the center of the grid stop participating in $F$'s transition process, as they remain in the "remaining agents" category, and $w_s = 0$.
4) As the agents move the object toward the left or right from its initial center position, it enters the penalty areas. To completely avoid them, the agents must learn to coordinate actions and keep the object in the center columns of the grid throughout an entire trial.
5) A penalty helps agents learn to avoid the left and right borders but also impacts the number of times agents at the borders play a role in the state transition (as agents coordinate actions to avoid those areas).

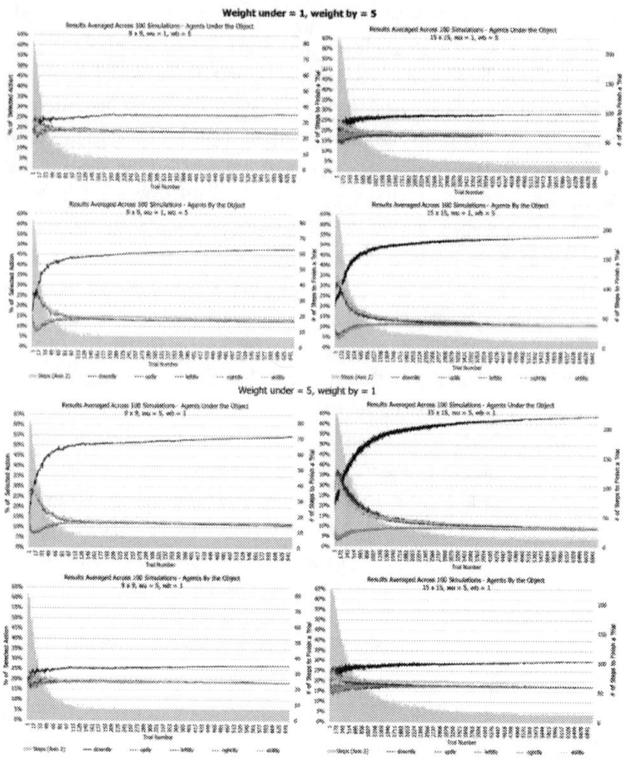


Figure 5. Upper level. Weights: $w_u = 1$, $w_b = 5$. Lower level. Weights: $w_u = 5$, $w_b = 1$. Over trials, the distribution of actions' percentage *per* agent category, and the number of steps taken to complete a trial. Left: $9 \times 9$ grid. Right: $15 \times 15$ grid. Results averaged across 100 simulations.

### A. *Results Across Grid Dimensions and Weights*

How do different grid dimensions and weights impact agent coordination? Figure 3 shows an overview/comparison across experiments: results depict, within the last recorded trial after convergence, the percentage of agents that selected the *down action*. Down is the optimal action if an enough number of agents continuously select down from the beginning until the end of a trial - which is expected to happen after convergence.

Figure 3 shows one data graphic *per* weight set, in the following order: $\{w_u = 1,\ w_b = 1\}$; and $\{w_u = 1,\ w_b = 5\}$; and $\{w_u = 3,\ w_b = 5\}$; and $\{w_u = 5,\ w_b = 1\}$; and $\{w_u = 5,\ w_b = 3\}$. We chose that ordering to facilitate visual comparison across flipped weights. Then, within each data graphic, the results across grid dimensions are split by agent category (if under or by the object).

We added boxes in Figure 3 to highlight experiments in which not all simulations converged to the optimal steps number within a trial (the optimal number is given by $N - n$): a dashed box means that simulations converged to [0, 3) more steps in relation to the optimal, a not-dashed box to [2, 7), and no box to [0, 1). You may ask: "Why are the final number of steps shown as ranges?" Our results are averaged across

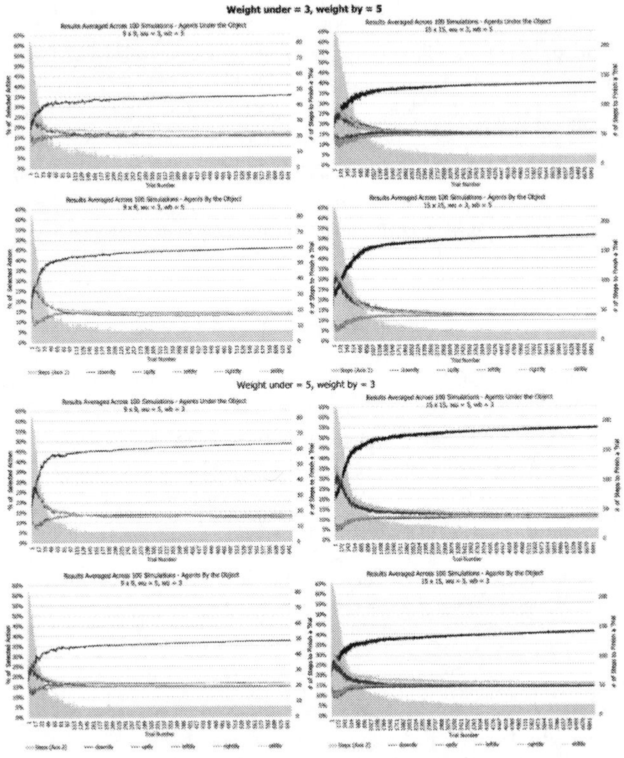


Figure 6. Upper level. Weights: $w_u = 3$, $w_b = 5$. Lower level. Weights: $w_u = 5$, $w_b = 3$. Over trials, the distribution of actions' percentage *per* agent category, and the number of steps taken to complete a trial. Left: $9 \times 9$ grid. Right: $15 \times 15$ grid. Results averaged across 100 simulations.

simulations and, similar to what the authors [2] observed in their experiments, not all learned policies are stable, and both lack of robustness against exploration and miscoordination penalties interfere with individual policies. As expected, these issues are more visible as we increase the size of the grid; for instance, $15 \times 15$, weights $w_u = w_b = 1$, and $w_u = 5$, $w_b = 3$ have the worst results: both converged to [2, 7) more steps than the minimum needed to accomplish the task.

Figure 3's upper level shows that when $w_u = w_b = 1$, agents select the down action with similar percentages. The remaining four graphics show that agent categories with higher weights facilitate their learning to select the optimal action. However, flipping weights lead to a slightly different distribution: observe when agents under the object have higher weight ($w_u = 5$, $w_b = 1$ and $w_u = 5$, $w_b = 3$) and compare it with when they have the lower weight ($w_u = 1$, $w_b = 5$ and $w_u = 3$, $w_b = 5$). If set to higher weights, more agents under the object learn to select the optimal action than would be the case for agents by the object. We suppose that happens due to a combination of the chosen parameters (such as the grid and object's dimensions) and the number of agents under the object (usually smaller than the number of agents by the object, see Figure 2) – therefore, making it easier for the agents under the object to learn to coordinate actions.

## B. *A Closer Look into the Grids* $15 \times 15$ *and* $9 \times 9$

In this section, we focus on Figures 4, 5, and 6. Here, we investigate our largest grid, $15 \times 15$, along with the most successful within the largest ones, $9 \times 9$ (by most successful, we mean that the object gets to the goal state within the minimum number of steps for all five sets of examined weights). For easy comparison, we always depict the results side by side: $9 \times 9$ at the left and $15 \times 15$ at the right. Each figure focuses on a set of weights: Figure 4 shows $w_u = w_b = 1$. Then, Figure 5 shows $w_u = 1, w_b = 5$ at the top, followed by $w_u = 5, w_b = 1$. Finally, Figure 6 shows $w_u = 3, w_b = 5$ at the top, followed by $w_u = 5, w_b = 3$. Here, we examine the action distribution within trials and across simulations to help check if/when the learned policies are close to the best policy. Therefore, Figures 4-6 depict the action distribution (down, up, left, right, still) over trials as well as the total number of steps within trials (we rounded the steps to the nearest whole number to facilitate visualization). Results are split by agent category: depicting first the agents *under the object*, followed by the agents *by the object*.

Given that agents always select an action per step within a trial, percentages are averaged within a trial and across simulations. To facilitate visualization, different grid dimensions have a distinct number of trials within each of the 100 simulations – this is why $15 \times 15$ shows a higher number of trials than $9 \times 9$ at the x-axis.

In Figure 4 only, we show the results for *the other agents* – we use a different background color to highlight a different scale, which was chosen to facilitate observation. However, we omit *the other agents* from Figures 5-6 since agents who are neither under nor by the object do not influence $F$'s transition process (since $w_s = 0$). Therefore, their action distribution remains within $1 \backslash (\#\text{of actions})$, or $1 \setminus 5$, which is $20\%$ *per* action, as Figure 4 shows. Due to the zero weight, actions from that agent category do not matter; consequently, they receive reinforcements in response to the actions of agents either under or by the object.

Overall, our results show that, as agents learn to select the down action, the number of steps used to successfully finish a trial diminishes: if not to the optimal number (given by $N-n$), to a number close to that (see Section IV-A). What is the main difference between Figures 4-6? Figure 4 shows that, in both grid dimensions, results for agents under and by the object are very similar – as one would expect given the identical weights.

Figure 5 shows a two-fold result: when agents by the object have higher weight ($w_u = 1$, $w_b = 5$), their percentages for the down action are higher; also, as one would expect, the opposite happens if we flip the weights ($w_u = 5$, $w_b = 1$). Finally, in Figure 6, although agents with higher weight still show higher percentages for the down action, this setting shows a higher overall selection for that action (under/by agents with more than $35\%$ to that action).

The DSSb is resourceful in investigating challenges faced by a large number of agents to coordinate actions in a Markov game; as the authors [2] point out, the DSSb "brings together action shadowing induced by penalties, Pareto-selection as there are several possibilities to reach the goal state". In fact, Figures 4-6 provide interesting examples of action shadowing. Still, before getting into action shadowing, let us visit the non-stationarity problem. As mentioned in the background section, independent learners ignore each others' presence and, therefore, can treat other agents as part of the environment. However, from each agent's perspective, the environment no longer appears Markovian and stationary since the "transition probabilities associated with the action of a single agent from one state to another are not stationary and change over time as the action choices of the other agents change. These choices are probably influenced by the past history of play, and so the history of play influences the future transition probabilities when revisiting a state" [2], [29].

Now, suppose agent $x$ selected an optimal action, while most of the other agents selected actions that move the object to a penalty area. Thus, the agent's $x$ action will be shadowed by a transition to a penalty area. Conversely, what happens if agent $x$ selects an action towards a penalty area while most agents select actions away from it? How can agent $x$ learn not to pick poor action choices? In Figures 4-6, note how the actions *l*eft and *r*ight drop initially as agents learn to avoid the penalty areas but then increase a bit. Once an enough number of agents coordinate actions and learn to avoid the penalty areas, it does not matter what agent $x$ selects. There is a point at which just enough agents learn the proper state/action pairs, impacting other agents' learning. To put it in simple terms, it is almost like a portion of agents at each step carries the entire team of agents one step closer to the goal. By looking into Figure 3, one may assume that higher percentages of agents always selecting the optimal action lead to better results overall. However, that is not completely true. Of course, enough agents need to select it so that the object moves to the goal state; however, once that happens, it does not matter how many more agents select that action. For instance, look at Figure 5, $9 \times 9$, weights $w_u = 5$, $w_b = 1$; the *d*own action keeps increasing, but trials are such that the optimum number of steps has already been reached. From an agent perspective, it should matter to learn the optimal state/action pairs; however, from a task perspective, successfully accomplishing it is likely to be the overall goal.

## V. Conclusion

In this paper, we first detail the Discrete Smart Surface benchmark while making a clear distinction between agent and environment. Then, we address the research questions listed in the Introduction and investigate the benchmark using various grid dimensions and agent weighting values – for example, we show how the distribution of actions per agent category varies over trials as agents learn to coordinate actions. Finally, the situated agents from DSSb offer important lessons for challenges in MAS; for instance, our experimental results contextualize and exemplify action shadowing, which we hope will be insightful for others investigating challenges in MAS. In future work, it would be interesting to study other grid dimensions, object shapes, and sizes, including different weighting systems (to contrast the roles of agents under *versus* by the object). The study would help to investigate questions, such as: if someone wanted to exploit the system and insert a number of agents with a fixed strategy only to deteriorate individual policies, what should be the minimum number of agents, and what grid cells should they occupy so as to maximize their effect?

## Acknowledgments

This work would not have been possible without the support from Grinnell College's Harris Faculty Fellowship and the Mentored Advanced Project (MAP) program.

* Authors' equal contributions.

## References

[1] S. Gronauer and K. Diepold, "Multi-agent deep reinforcement learning: a survey," *Artificial Intelligence Review*, pp. 1–49, 2022.

[2] L. Matignon, G. J. Laurent, and N. Le Fort-Piat, "Independent reinforcement learners in cooperative markov games: a survey regarding coordination problems," *The Knowledge Engineering Review*, vol. 27, no. 1, pp. 1–31, 2012.

[3] J. E. Luntz, W. Messner, and H. Choset, "Distributed manipulation using discrete actuator arrays," *The International Journal of Robotics Research*, vol. 20, no. 7, pp. 553–583, 2001.

[4] M. L. Littman, "Markov games as a framework for multi-agent reinforcement learning," in *Proceedings of the Eleventh International Conference on International Conference on Machine Learning*, ser. ICML'94. San Francisco, CA, USA: Morgan Kaufmann Publishers Inc., 1994, p. 157–163.

[5] M. Benda, V. Jagannathan, and R. Dodhiawala, "On optimal cooperation of knowledge sources-an experimental investigation," *Boeing Advanced Technology Center, Boeing Computing Services, Seattle, Washington, Tech. Rep. BCS-G2010-280*, 1986.

[6] D. Weyns, G. Vizzari, and T. Holvoet, "Environments for situated multi-agent systems: Beyond infrastructure," in *Environments for Multi-Agent Systems II: Second International Workshop, E4MAS 2005, Utrecht, The Netherlands, July 25, 2005, Selected Revised and Invited Papers 2*. Springer, 2006, pp. 1–17.

[7] E. H. Durfee and T. A. Montgomery, "Mice: A flexible testbed for intelligent coordination experiments," in *Proceedings of the 1989 Distributed Artificial Intelligence Workshop*, 1989, pp. 25–40.

[8] S. Sukhbaatar, A. Szlam, and R. Fergus, "Learning multiagent communication with backpropagation," *30th Conference on Neural Information Processing Systems (NIPS)*, vol. 29, pp. 2252–2260, 2016.

[9] M. Hausknecht, P. Mupparaju, S. Subramanian, S. Kalyanakrishnan, and P. Stone, "Half field offense: An environment for multiagent learning and ad hoc teamwork," in *AAMAS Adaptive Learning Agents (ALA) Workshop*, Singapore, May 2016.

[10] M. Kim, J. Oh, Y. Lee, J. Kim, S. Kim, S. Chong, and S.-Y. Yun, "The starcraft multi-agent challenges+: Learning of multi-stage tasks and environmental factors without precise reward functions," *arXiv preprint arXiv:2207.02007*, 2022.

[11] J. E. Luntz, W. Messner, and H. Choset, "Parcel manipulation and dynamics with a distributed actuator array: the virtual vehicle," in *Proceedings of International Conference on Robotics and Automation*, vol. 2, 1997, pp. 1541–1546 vol.2.

[12] F. Cicirelli, A. Giordano, and L. Nigro, "Efficient environment management for distributed simulation of large-scale situated multi-agent systems," *Concurrency and Computation: Practice and Experience*, vol. 27, no. 3, pp. 610–632, 2015.

[13] D. Weyns, H. Van Dyke Parunak, F. Michel, T. Holvoet, and J. Ferber, "Environments for multiagent systems state-of-the-art and research challenges," in *Environments for Multi-Agent Systems: First International Workshop, E4MAS 2004, LNAI 3374*. Springer, 2005, pp. 1–47.

[14] T. W. Malone and K. Crowston, "What is coordination theory and how can it help design cooperative work systems?" in *Proceedings of the 1990 ACM conference on Computer-supported cooperative work*, 1990, pp. 357–370.
[15] A. Consoli, J. Tweedale, and L. Jain, "The link between agent coordination and cooperation," in *Intelligent Information Processing III: IFIP TC12 International Conference on Intelligent Information Processing (IIP 2006), September 20–23, Adelaide, Australia 3*. Springer, 2007, pp. 11–19.
[16] M. Tan, "Multi-agent reinforcement learning: Independent vs. cooperative agents," in *Proceedings of the tenth international conference on machine learning*, 1993, pp. 330–337.
[17] J. Stüber, C. Zito, and R. Stolkin, "Let's push things forward: A survey on robot pushing," *Frontiers in Robotics and AI*, p. 8, 2020.
[18] D. E. Acuña and P. Schrater, "Structure learning in human sequential decision-making," *PLOS Computational Biology*, vol. 6, no. 12, pp. 1–12, 2010.
[19] L. Matignon, L. Jeanpierre, and A.-I. Mouaddib, "Coordinated multi-robot exploration under communication constraints using decentralized markov decision processes," in *Proceedings of the AAAI Conference on Artificial Intelligence*, vol. 26, no. 1, 2012, pp. 2017–2023.
[20] C. Claus and C. Boutilier, "The dynamics of reinforcement learning in cooperative multiagent systems," *AAAI/IAAI*, vol. 1998, no. 746-752, p. 2, 1998.
[21] R. S. Sutton and A. G. Barto, *Reinforcement learning: An introduction (2nd ed.)*. MIT press, 2018 [1998].
[22] C. J. Watkins, "Learning from delayed rewards," 1989.
[23] C. Boutilier, "Sequential optimality and coordination in multiagent systems," in *IJCAI'99: Proceedings of the 16th international joint conference on Artificial intelligence*, vol. 1, 1999, pp. 478–485.
[24] L. Peshkin, K.-E. Kim, N. Meuleau, and L. P. Kaelbling, "Learning to cooperate via policy search," *arXiv preprint cs/0105032*, 2001.
[25] J. J. Gibson, *The senses considered as perceptual systems*. Bloomsbury Academic, 1966.
[26] ——, *The Ecological Approach to Visual Perception: Classic Edition*. Psychology Press, 1979.
[27] C. S. Horstmann, *Core Java: Fundamentals, Volume 1*. Pearson Education, 2022.
[28] C. J. Watkins and P. Dayan, "Q-learning," *Machine learning*, vol. 8, pp. 279–292, 1992.
[29] M. Bowling and M. Veloso, *An analysis of stochastic game theory for multiagent reinforcement learning*. Tech. rep., Computer Science Department, Carnegie Mellon University, 2000.

# Vessel Route Planning Optimization Combined with Time Windows versus Worker Scheduling for Offshore Windmill Maintenance

E. De Kuyffer, L. Martens, W. Joseph, T. De Pessemier
Department of Information Technology
Ghent University/IMEC
Ghent, Belgium
e-mail: Erik.DeKuyffer@UGent.be, Luc1.Martens@UGent.be, Wout.Joseph@UGent.be, Toon.DePessemier@UGent.be

*Abstract*—**The high fuel prices and the important costs associated with windmill downtime during maintenance urge the need to minimize travel time and scheduling of jobs in a short time period. Since landing in windmills at sea is difficult and depends on meteorological parameters, the constraint of maintenance windows is added when searching for the optimal route. To minimize the distance traveled, the Vehicle Routing Problem with Time Windows (VRPTW) is solved, using three different methods. The VRPTW is applied to two separate databases, namely various sets of windmills to be maintained and several numbers of customers to be serviced. Applications with 8 to 175 windmills, divided over 3 farms have shown that the VRPTW solved by using three different methods resulted in a similar relative gain in travel distance, compared to a randomly chosen route. The main difference between the methods studied is the amount of calculation time needed, which varies from 1 second to 6 minutes for the different methods. To demonstrate the general applicability, the same three methods were executed on a set of service tasks performed at 8 to 40 customers of a window decoration company, distributed throughout Belgium, resulting in similar outcomes. In a second part of the paper, the Job Shop Scheduling Problem (JSSP) is solved to minimize the total maintenance span of offshore windmills as an additional objective function. This led to a relative gain of up to 62% in maintenance time, compared to the total maximum maintenance span for an application of 40 windmills. Finally, both objectives, minimal distance and minimal maintenance time span, are combined, resulting in a set of non-dominated maintenance sequences that can be used by the planner.**

***Keywords-VRPTW; VRPy; OR Tools; ACO; Job Shop Scheduling; Pareto.***

## I. INTRODUCTION

Due to high fuel prices and significant labor costs, it is extremely important to limit the distance covered and the time consumed for offshore windmill maintenance. This paper focuses on the reduction of regular maintenance and repair costs. Vessel routing optimization for offshore windmill maintenance thereby is a very complex problem. It has been the topic of recent studies [1]–[4]. To demonstrate the general applicability of the VRPTW to obtain minimal distance routes and to show that all three methods studied - VRPy, Operational Research (OR) Tools and Ant Colony Optimization (ACO) - lead to similar results for other data sets, the procedures are applied to the discrete product installation planning. The interventions of companies that distribute and maintain unique products per customer - the so-called Value Added Resellers or VARs - can be split in the installation of the products and ad hoc maintenance of previously installed products. The planning of the delivery and installation can be considered as proactive planning, allowing optimization of the distance to be traveled, and thus the amount of fuel used. Maintenance interventions are more reactive of nature, making optimal planning more difficult. In a second part of this paper, we focus on reducing downtime by arranging maintenance jobs in such a way that the total service time span is minimized. To obtain this objective, the Job Shop Scheduling Problem (JSSP) is solved, in which the machines are replaced by workers. For each worker, a sequence is calculated so that all maintenance jobs are executed within a limited time frame, reducing the total downtime of all the windmills that need service. Finally, both objectives are applied to the same set of windmills, resulting in a Pareto front of non-dominated solutions offered to the planner to choose from (Section V). It will become clear from the list of these Pareto points that reaching both objectives at the same time is nearly infeasible, and thus the optimal sequence must be chosen out of this list of non-dominated solutions.

The novelties of this paper are: (i) the comparison of three solution methods for the vehicle routing problem with time windows applied to windmill maintenance vessels and to discrete product installation and service, (ii) the combined windmill sequence travel distance and maintenance time span optimization by solving both the VRPTW and the JSSP on the same data set, and (iii) the importance of reaching both objectives in maintenance cost reduction.

The remainder of the paper is organized as follows. In Section II, references are made to related work and Section III describes the problem formulation. The three methods used to solve the Vehicle Routing Problem with Time Windows, as well as the solution method for the JSSP are listed in Section IV. Section V lists the results of all the optimization methods discussed for VRPTW and JSSP and compares both by calculating the corresponding Pareto points. Finally, Sections VI and VII contain an evaluation of the results and provide a conclusion, respectively.

## II. RELATED WORK

The Vehicle Routing Problem (VRP) was first investigated more than six decades ago. This routing problem initiated major developments in the fields of exact algorithms and heuristics [5]. The vehicle routing problem comprises the design of least cost delivery routes through a set of geographically dispersed locations, subject to one or more side constraints.

Constraints to vehicle routing problems linked to capacity result in the Capacitated Vehicle Routing Problem (CVRP). If a time window is added to each location, asset, or customer, we talk about VRPTW [6]. In addition to the capacity constraint, a vehicle in the VRPTW has to visit a location, asset, or customer within a certain time frame. The vehicle - car, vessel, or other - is allowed to arrive before the time window opens, but the customer or asset cannot be serviced until the respective time window opens. In addition, it is not allowed to arrive after the time window has closed [7]. The different solution methodologies for the VRP can be divided into three categories: Exact methods, heuristics, and meta-heuristics. The exact methods generate optimal solutions and guarantee their optimality. This method class includes a variety of approaches, mainly branch and X (X being cut, bound, price, etc.), dynamic programming, and column generation methods. The heuristics aim to methodically find an acceptable solution within a limited number of iterations. Metaheuristics can finally be defined as a class of heuristics that search beyond the local optima if they exist [8]. Research papers on VRP, with or without time windows, are quite common, since their application in daily life is widely spread, for example, in the delivery of packages and the route planning of nurses [9]–[12]. The principle of using VRPTW to optimize offshore wind farm maintenance routes for multiple vessels has never been applied.

In addition, extensive research has been done on maintenance and production scheduling according to the flow shop method, as well as the job shop method in different industries [13]–[15]. Al-Shayea et al. designed a model to integrate production scheduling and maintenance planning for flow-shop production systems. This model is based on the optimal job sequence that will be processed on several connected machines in series. The objective of this study is to find the optimal sequence of jobs, while reducing total production and maintenance costs [16]. None of the papers apply, however, to maintenance scheduling in windmill farms, while costs for this is very high, and every hour of downtime (due to maintenance) results in an important loss of revenue.

## III. PROBLEM FORMULATION

### A. Experimental Design - VRPTW

The goal of solving the VRPTW will be to find the optimal maintenance or installation sequence to minimize the total distance traveled, with a minimal number of vessels, taking into account that some maintenance tasks can only be serviced for a certain period of time. For both data sets, the load is never an issue, neither for the vessels that only need to transport maintenance people nor for the vans that are big enough to carry all products that need to be installed in one day. Finally, both data sets are directly obtained from the windmill maintenance company and the window decoration value added reseller, and no prefiltering or preprocessing was done, except a random selection of a predefined batch out of the total set, ranging from 8 to 175 windmills and from 8 to 40 VAR customers.

Figure 1 shows an example of a windmill configuration after applying the VRP solution method with time windows.

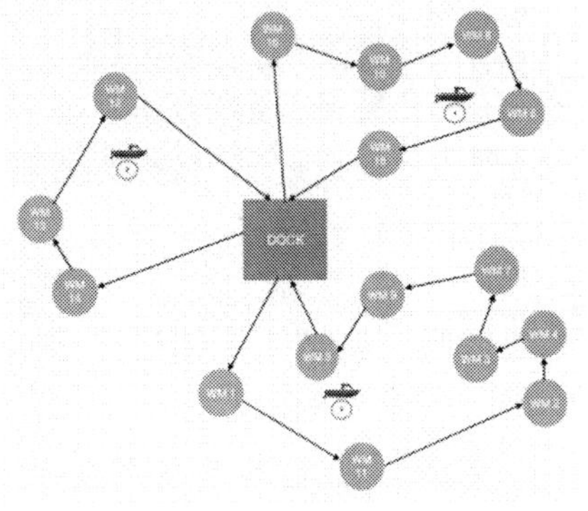


Figure 1. Optimal windmill service routes after solving the VRP.

The configuration used in this example has one dock and 16 windmills spread over three farms to be serviced. The different windmills are indicated as $WM_i$ (i = 1-16), where each windmill must be visited exactly once. Solving the VRP leads to three routes that three different vessels must take, as shown in Figure 1. The fact that more than one vessel is necessary to service all windmills is caused by the time windows in which maintenance of a windmill needs to be carried out. A similar configuration can be set up for the customers of a Value Added Reseller, where the windmills are then replaced by customers to be visited for installation or maintenance of discrete products.

### B. Experimental Design - JSSP

In a typical scheduling problem in the job shop, different jobs are scheduled on multiple machines to minimize the total production time [14][15]. However, for this research paper, we replaced the machines on which the work is performed by workers that manually execute the maintenance jobs. For each worker, the sequence of jobs is optimized in such a way that the total work span is minimized. Each job is represented by a different shade of color, and the size of the blocks corresponds to the amount of time it costs to complete the maintenance task. The workflow of a job shop is complex because it is different for every job. In this paper, the job shop scheduling will be discussed as it is a good match with the maintenance jobs scheduling for offshore windmill maintenance, making it the first time, according to the author's knowledge, the JSSP is used for maintenance planning of offshore windmills.

Figure 2 shows an example of a job sequence per worker obtained by solving the JSSP for a group of 16 windmills spread over 3 farms. The number of workers is set to three on the vertical axis, in analogy with the number of machines in the original JSSP used in a production environment. In each windmill, one worker needs to perform a service task and each worker needs to perform several maintenance tasks in separate windmills. Applying the JSSP solver to this configuration leads to an optimal sequence in which each worker needs to perform service on the windmills (s)he is responsible for, with a different service time on each windmill, shown on the horizontal axis. Thus, for each worker, a sequence of jobs is

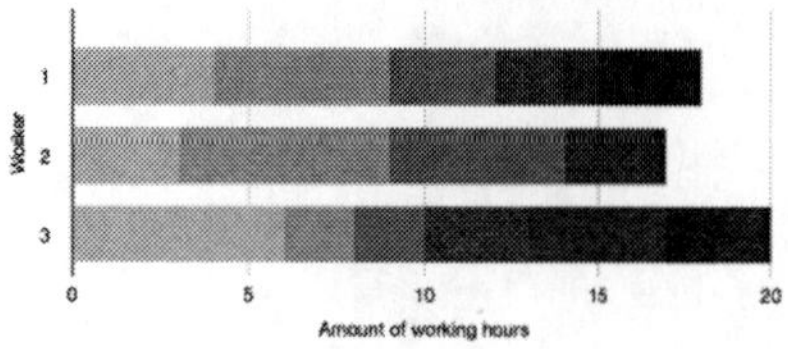


Figure 2. Optimal windmill service job sequence for 3 workers and different colored jobs of various length after solving the JSSP.

shown, each corresponding with a different color and with a size in accordance with the length of the job.

### C. Output Parameters

The output parameters for the VRPTW problem are the optimal number of vessels or trucks, the optimal sequence, and the travel time for each vessel or truck in minutes. Furthermore, the relative gain in travel time ($\Delta G_t$) is calculated by dividing a randomly chosen travel time ($TTt|Random$) minus the Total Travel time (TTt) by a randomly chosen travel time (see (1)). The output parameters for the JSSP problem are an optimized sequence of maintenance tasks per worker to minimize Total Downtime (TDt). This is then compared to the total time needed for one worker ($TDt|OneWorker$) and a relative gain is calculated ($\Delta G_w$) by using (2).

$$\Delta G_t = 100 \cdot \frac{TTt|Random - TTt}{TTt|Random}(\%) \tag{1}$$

$$\Delta G_w = 100 \cdot \frac{TDt|OneWorker - TDt}{TDt|OneWorker}(\%) \tag{2}$$

## IV. Method

### A. Solution method - VRPTW

In this paper, three methods are discussed, namely VRPy, a tool that uses a Column Generation Approach (CGA) [17], the OR Tools solver, developed by Google Operational Research [11], and an ACO algorithm, a metaheuristic solving method [18]. Table I summarizes the three methods and describes their characteristics. While VRPy takes (much longer) to arrive at a result, especially for large datasets, OR Tools generates a result almost instantaneously but of slightly less quality. These conclusions are numerically confirmed in Tables II and III. All calculations are done on a MacBook Pro from 2021 with the new Apple M1 chip and 8Mb RAM.

TABLE I
COMPARISON OF ALL METHODS USED TO SOLVE THE VRPTW

| Method | Advantage | Disadvantage |
|---|---|---|
| VRPy | Easy Interface | Less Powerful |
| OR Tools | Fast and Accurate | No optimal result |
| ACO | Optimal results | No Easy Interface |

To calculate the distances between the windmills or customers and between the starting point and the windmills or customers, spherical trigonometry formulas are used. In this paper, all vehicles are considered the same: they have the same velocity, the same capacity, and unit freight. Furthermore, the capacity and cargo of the vessel are not considered constraints.

When defining $t_i$ as the time it takes for the vessel to arrive at location i, e as the cost of waiting and f as the cost of arriving too late, the objective of solving the VRPTW for a collection of vehicles A, can be written as:

$$min(\sum_{i=0}^{N}\sum_{j=0}^{N}\sum_{a=1}^{A} x_{ija}*d_{ij}+\sum_{i=1}^{N} max\{e*(m_{bi}-t_i); 0; f*(t_i-m_{ei})\} \tag{3}$$

Where:

$$x_{ija} = \begin{cases} 1 & \text{if the vehicle a travels from i to j,} \\ 0 & \text{in all other cases} \end{cases} \tag{4}$$

$$t_{ija} = \sum x_{ija}(t_i + \frac{d_{ij}}{v} + s_i) \quad (t_0 = 0, s_0 = 0) \tag{5}$$

The constraints are:

$$\sum_{j=1}^{N}\sum_{a=1}^{A} x_{jia} = \sum_{j=1}^{N}\sum_{a=1}^{A} x_{ija} = A \quad (i = 0) \tag{6}$$

$$\sum_{j=0}^{N}\sum_{a=1}^{A} x_{ija} = 1 \quad (i \in N) \tag{7}$$

$$\sum_{i=0}^{N}\sum_{a=1}^{A} x_{ija} = 1 \quad (j \in N) \tag{8}$$

$$\sum_{j=1}^{N} x_{ija} = \sum_{j=1}^{N} x_{jia} = 1 \quad (i = 0 \quad a \in A) \tag{9}$$

In (3), the second part of the equation - sum of maximums - defines the time window constraint. In (5), $t_{ija}$ is the time it takes the vehicle to travel from location i to j, v is the speed and $s_i$ the service at location i. At the depot (node 0 in the equations), both t and s are equal to zero. The constraint in (6) implies that the number of vehicles that start from the loading point and go back there is A. Constraints (7) and (8) mean that each location can be visited only by one vehicle. Finally, constraint (9) represents that all the vehicles that start from the loading point also go back there. VRPy solves the vehicle routing problem with a column generation approach [17]. The term refers to the fact that, continuously, routes are generated with a pricing problem and fed to a master problem. The latter selects the best routes among a pool so that each node (windmill or customer in this case) is serviced exactly once. The pricing problem is actually a shortest elementary path problem. Additional constraints, such as the time windows discussed in this paper, contribute to a shortest-path problem with resource constraints. VRPy does not lead to an optimal solution, even without time limits. Hence, when solving pricing problems does not result in a route with negative marginal cost, the master problem is solved as mixed integer programming. This price-and-branch strategy does not guarantee an ideal solution.

Next, the above solution will be compared with the results found for the same operational VRPTW using the solver developed for Google OR Tools (Table I) [11]. The algorithm based on the Python routing library wrapper results in a new set of optimal routes, taking into consideration that all windmills or customers need to be serviced in a specific time frame. As for the first method, no other restrictions are taken into account. The algorithm used to solve VRPTW starts with the creation of input data, followed by a callback function. After adding the time constraints, the default search parameters and a heuristic method are set for the first solution. Finally, the same function is used to solve the Traveling Salesman Problem (TSP), resulting in the route for each vehicle, the total travel time of the vehicle route, and the solution windows of each location. The solution window at a location is defined as the time interval during which a vehicle must arrive, so it stays on schedule.

The third method to solve the VRPTW with the same entry data - like position of the windmills or customers, service windows - is based on an ant colony optimization algorithm [4], [18]. Ant Colony Optimization (ACO) is one of the most recent metaheuristic approaches to combinatorial optimization problems. The pseudocode is shown below. All three solution methods, VRPy, OR Tools, and ACO are heuristic methods. When it is impossible or impractical to find an optimal solution, heuristic methods can be used to accelerate the process of discovering a satisfactory solution. These heuristics can be described as strategies derived from previous experiences with similar problems.

**procedure** ACO Meta-Heuristic **is**
    **while not** terminated **do**
        ConstructAntsSolutions()
        UpdatePheromones()
        daemonActions()
    **repeat**
**end procedure**

ACO is based on the foraging behavior of real ants. They arbitrarily explore the environment, using pheromone deposits to find the shortest routes. Therefore, ACO algorithms are probabilistic techniques suitable for solving optimization problems that aim at minimizing the distance traveled (e.g., TSP and VRP). In the first step - *ConstructAntsSolutions* - of the algorithm, each artificial ant generates a solution: thereby it randomly chooses the next city to visit, based on a heuristic combination of the distance to that city and the amount of virtual pheromone left behind on the arc to that city. The ants explore and dump pheromone on each arc they traverse until they have all completed a tour (see (10)). At this point, the ant that has completed the shortest tour deposits virtual pheromone along its complete route (*UpdatePheromones*). Equation (14) shows that the amount of pheromone deposited is inversely proportional to the length of the tour. Thus, the shorter the route, the more pheromone the ant deposits on the arcs of the corresponding tour. The *deamonActions* procedure is used to carry out centralized actions that cannot be carried out by individual ants, as they do not possess global knowledge. A typical example of these *deamonActions* is the collection of global information that can be used to decide whether it might be useful to deposit additional pheromone to bias the search process from a nonlocal perspective. As long as the termination condition is not met, these three steps are repeated [19]. The pheromone $\tau_{ij}$, associated with the edge joining locations i and j, is updated as follows:

$$\tau_{ij} \leftarrow (1-\rho)\tau_{ij} + \sum_{k=1}^{m} \Delta\tau_{ij}^{k} \quad (10)$$

where:

$$\rho = \text{evaporation rate}, \quad (11)$$

$$m = \text{number of ants}, \quad (12)$$

$$\Delta\tau_{ij}^{k} = \text{the quantity of pheromone laid on edge (i, j) by ant k}, \quad (13)$$

$$\Delta\tau_{ij}^{k} = \begin{cases} \frac{Q}{L_k} & \text{if ant k used edge (i,j) in its tour,} \\ 0 & \text{in all other cases} \end{cases} \quad (14)$$

$$Q = \text{a constant}, \quad (15)$$

$$L_k = \text{is the length of the tour built by ant k}, \quad (16)$$

To determine and confirm that the solutions obtained by the three methods to solve VRPTW are applicable in other areas, the same solution procedures were applied to two data sets. In addition to windmill farms, a data set is used consisting of the customer coordinates at which discrete Taylormade products (curtains) are to be installed and maintained. Although this data set differs quite extensively from that of the windmills, the optimization goals are the same, namely travel time, and thus fuel consumption reduction. Transport for Taylormade products goes over land and cannot follow a straight line, the distances between customers are smaller than for the windmill farms (typically a few tens of kilometers versus a few hundreds for the windmills) and not clustered around different farms, making the data sets for windmills and customers quite different.

### *B. Solution Method - Job shop*

To apply the solver to maintenance planning, we have made the following assumptions: the machines in the JSSP are replaced by the workers performing maintenance jobs (the job is a sequence of windmills to be serviced), and the tasks are linked to the windmills. The processing time is chosen randomly, as are the workers for each maintenance job. The final result of the algorithm created to solve the JSSP will be a schedule optimized for each worker to minimize the total maintenance span. Figure 3 shows the building blocks of the algorithm used to solve JSSP with the OR solver.

Each of the steps in the flow chart are further defined as:

- Data Creation: For each maintenance job, several tasks are defined, that is, the windmills or customers to be serviced. For every windmill or customer, the worker that needs to perform the task and the service time needed are given.
- Declaration of the model, a Constraint Programming (CP) model that includes variables and constraints that will be solved via the CP solver.

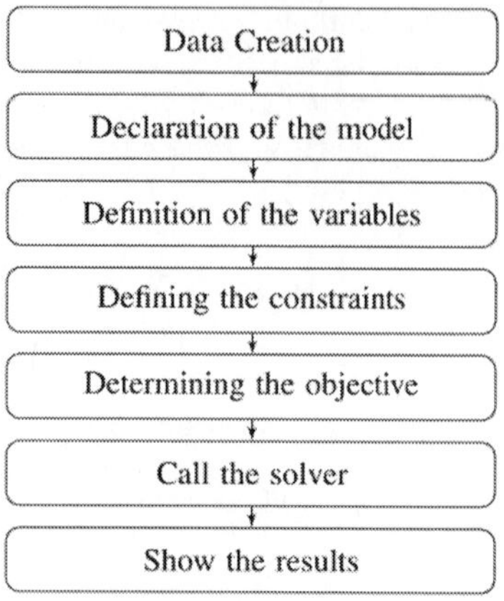


Figure 3. Flow Diagram of the JSSP solution method.

- Definition of the variables, which are the start and end time, the duration (end minus start) and the interval of the task.
- Defining the constraints: A worker cannot work at two windmills at the same time, plus the condition that, for any two consecutive tasks in the same maintenance job, the first must be completed before the second can be started.
- Determining the objective as the minimization of the make span.
- Call the solver and show the results.

The objective function (17) and the constraints of the job shop scheduling problem are written as:

$$min\ C_S \tag{17}$$

where:

$$C_{1j} - w_{1j} = r_j + p_{1j} \qquad \forall j \tag{18}$$

$$C_{i-1j} - C_{ij} + w_{ij} = -p_{ij} \qquad i = 2, ..., m_j, \quad \forall j \tag{19}$$

$$C_{ik} - C_{ij} \geq p_{ik} \quad \text{or} \quad C_{ij} - C_{ik} \geq p_{ij} \quad \forall i, \quad \forall j, k \in J_i \tag{20}$$

$$C_{ij}, w_{ij} \geq 0 \quad i = 1, ..., m_j \quad \forall j \tag{21}$$

Constraint (18) implies that a maintenance job can only start after its respective ready time. Constraint (19) specifies that a job j follows its processing sequence. The machine capacity constraint (20) finally ensures that a worker can process only one operation at a time, and an operation will be finished once it starts.

### C. Pareto front

Solving the VRPTW and JSSP leads to sequences in which windmills or customers need to be visited, each with a different objective function. Hence, for the VRPTW, the objective is to minimize the total distance traveled, while the JSSP attempts to reduce the total maintenance time. Since both objectives are possibly contradictory, the solution methods are compared by calculating Pareto points and a corresponding Pareto front. Therefore, the maintenance sequences resulting from the VRPTW, with a minimal route distance, are offered to the second objective function to calculate the corresponding total maintenance time. Additionally, maintenance sequences with minimal maintenance are calculated by solving the JSSP and the corresponding total route distance is determined. Both lead to a set of two-dimensional coordinates of which the Pareto points are calculated. Pareto optimal points are non-dominated, meaning that there does not exist another solution that rigorously dominates the Pareto optimal solution in terms of any objective. The Pareto front is the multi-objective and multi-dimensional alternative for the individual optimal solution resulting from single objective optimisation problems (VRP and JSSP).

## V. RESULTS

### A. Sequence comparison VRPy - OR Tools - ACO for windmill maintenance

Table II lists the best results obtained by applying all three solution methods, and this for different configurations, ranging from 8 to 175 windmills. The relative gain shows how much better the optimized solution is than the randomly chosen one. The optimal number of vessels proposed by the VRPTW solvers is shown in the Vessel column, and finally the Runtime column lists the time needed to solve the VRPTW problem. For VRPy and OR Tools, the same sequence was obtained when running 10 tests for each. With ACO, the best result represents the shortest routes obtained after 20 tests, with 50 ants and 1000 iterations. The randomly selected route is considered identical and is expressed in minutes of travel time for the maintenance vessels. The values correspond to the total travel time of all vessels used in the maintenance schedule. Applying VRPy on a selection of 16 windmills to be maintained, to solve the Vehicle Routing Problem with time constraints, leads to a relative gain compared to the randomly chosen route of a little more than 44%. To obtain this minimal total travel time, three vessels need to be deployed simultaneously, each following a separate route.

Table II shows that the three solution methods, VRPy, OR Tools, and ACO, lead to an almost equal relative gain compared to a random route time of all vessels involved. This accounts for all configurations, varying from 8 to 40 windmills, and increases gradually as the number of windmills to be maintained grows. Except for the configuration of 8 Windmills, the number of vessels proposed by each method are the same, making comparison easier. The only significant difference between the VRPTW solvers is the calculation time required to obtain an optimized solution. Although the average calculation time for the smallest configuration is almost zero and comparable for all options, it rises very fast - almost exponentially - for the VRPy solution, up to more than 350 seconds for the 40 windmills. The calculation time of the ACO algorithm also increases, but is linear and thus not as distinct as for the VRPy solution method. OR Tools finally results in a set of optimized routes instantaneously, even for the set of 40 windmills.

Table II further contains the results obtained using the three VRPTW solution procedures for a large set of 175 windmills. For this sample, there is a (very) high relative gain for all three solvers, but also a significant difference between the yields obtained by VRPy and OR Tools and that by ACO. Although

TABLE II
OPTIMIZATION RESULTS FOR ALL METHODS FOR DIFFERENT WM CONFIGURATIONS

| Method | Rel gain (%) | Vessels | Run-time (sec) |
|---|---|---|---|
| | 8 Windmills | | |
| VRPy | 11.8% | 3 | 0.33 |
| OR Tools | 16.6% | 2 | 0.03 |
| ACO | 16.6% | 2 | 1.23 |
| | 16 Windmills | | |
| VRPy | 44.1% | 3 | 1.59 |
| OR Tools | 44.1% | 3 | 0.04 |
| ACO | 44.0% | 3 | 2.87 |
| | 24 Windmills | | |
| VRPy | 68.3% | 3 | 10.02 |
| OR Tools | 68.4% | 3 | 0.05 |
| ACO | 68.3% | 3 | 4.52 |
| | 32 Windmills | | |
| VRPy | 70.2% | 3 | 70.61 |
| OR Tools | 70.3% | 3 | 0.12 |
| ACO | 70.2% | 3 | 7.67 |
| | 40 Windmills | | |
| VRPy | 77.3% | 3 | 351.39 |
| OR Tools | 77.3% | 3 | 0.09 |
| ACO | 76.3% | 3 | 19.71 |
| | 175 Windmills | | |
| VRPy | 91.4% | 3 | >24h |
| **OR Tools** | **91.7%** | **3** | **3.51** |
| ACO | 81.2% | 9 | 507.50 |

not negligible, the calculation time for OR Tools is only 3.5 seconds, while ACO now requires more than 8 minutes to obtain a much worse result for a larger number of vessels. VRPy takes an extremely long time to get to a set of optimized routes.

TABLE III
OPTIMIZATION RESULTS FOR ALL METHODS FOR DIFFERENT CUSTOMER CONFIGURATIONS

| Method | Rel gain (%) | Vessels | Runtime (sec) |
|---|---|---|---|
| | 8 Customers | | |
| VRPy | 29.1% | 3 | 0.45 |
| OR Tools | 28.7% | 3 | 0.03 |
| ACO | 28.8% | 3 | 2.04 |
| | 16 Customers | | |
| VRPy | 52.5% | 4 | 1.70 |
| OR Tools | 52.9% | 3 | 0.03 |
| ACO | 52.1% | 4 | 2.98 |
| | 24 Customers | | |
| VRPy | 65.0% | 3 | 11.53 |
| OR Tools | 59.9% | 3 | 0.04 |
| ACO | 63.4% | 4 | 6.64 |
| | 32 Customers | | |
| VRPy | 64.8% | 3 | 47.93 |
| OR Tools | 64.8% | 3 | 0.09 |
| ACO | 62.8% | 4 | 7.89 |
| | 40 Customers | | |
| VRPy | 70.5% | 4 | 70.09 |
| **OR Tools** | **70.3%** | **4** | **0.12** |
| ACO | 64.1% | 4 | 11.08 |

### *B. Sequence comparison VRPy - OR Tools - ACO for customer interventions*

The same solution methods were applied to another data set. This set contains the coordinates of customers of a company that performs interventions on site. These clients are distributed throughout Belgium and are chosen at random from the company's database. The main difference with the windmill configuration is the way the locations are spread: while the windmills are grouped in three so-called parks, the customers are scattered throughout the Belgian territory.

Table III shows that the relative gain obtained by the OR solver, VRPy and ACO is again increasing as the number of customers to be served grows. Also, the conclusions about the calculation times are similar to those made for the windmill case: very limited for OR Tools, being almost instantaneously; slightly increasing for the ACO algorithm, ranging from 2 seconds for 8 customers up to 11 seconds for 40 customers and evolving in a more or less linear way; and finally more largely increasing for VRPy, from less than 1 second for 8 to over 70 seconds for 40 customers, following a more exponential curve. However, there are some important differences. First, there are slightly larger gaps between the relative gain obtained for every solution method, while for the windmill case, the results are nearly equal. This is probably due to the fact that there is a clustering around the different farms, making it easier for each method to get stuck in local minima much faster in the previously discussed windmill case. In the taylormade data set, there is no clustering and thus this phenomenon does not arise. Second, the optimal number of vehicles is not always equal for each solution, making the comparison more difficult.

### *C. Job Shop - Workers and windmill maintenance combined*

Table IV shows the results of the tests with a different number of windmills, divided over 3 separate farms, ranging from 8 to 40 assets. If all maintenance jobs would be carried out consecutively by one worker without waiting time - being the worst-case scenario for the total maintenance time span - the total time span for all jobs would be 18h for 8 windmills and 120h for 40 windmills. However, if we optimize the schedule for more workers, the total time span would be much lower, being 11 hours for 2 workers in the 8 windmills configuration and 45h for 6 workers in the 40 windmills configuration. This corresponds to a relative gain in maintenance time of respectively around 39% and 62% in the total maintenance time span with respect to the single worker case. By employing more workers simultaneously, the total maintenance time lost is (more than) halved, and therefore downtime is reduced by (more than) 50%. Although the total number of working hours is higher when using three workers instead of one, the amount of money gained by halving the downtime is significantly higher, hence the huge advantage of the JSSP solver. According to the average price per kWh in December 2022, the loss per windmill for 1h downtime is at least 203€ per hour if we presume that a windmill operates 24h per day, 365 days per year. A reduction of the downtime by 67h (with 3 workers) thus leads to a cost reduction of more than 13.6K Euro per windmill. If we further estimate the average labor cost per worker at 60 euros per hour and compare the total amount of hours worked by three workers (154 hours) with the 120 hours needed for one worker, then the extra costs would be 34 times 60 euros, or 2K euros. The net gain would then be 13.6K minus 2K, thus 11.6K.

TABLE IV
JSSP OPTIMIZATION BY USING OR TOOLS

| Use Case | Relative gain |
|---|---|
| 08 Windmills - 2 workers | 38,9% |
| 16 Windmills - 3 workers | 48,7% |
| 24 Windmills - 4 workers | 53,8% |
| 32 Windmills - 5 workers | 59,6% |
| 40 Windmills - 6 workers | 62,5% |

Table V shows that in the 40 windmill configuration, the largest downtime gain is obtained when switching from one to two workers (44%) and a much lower but significant gain when switching to three workers. From 4 workers onwards, the total maintenance time span does not lower very much when adding extra workers. The trade-off can thus be put at 4 workers or, when labor is expensive, at 3 workers. Remark that when using as many workers as there are tasks to perform, the relative gain is obtained by dividing the longest task by the total time for all tasks, and thus results in a very high optimization (95% in our case).

TABLE V
JSSP OPTIMIZATION IN FUNCTION OF THE NUMBER OF WORKERS FOR 40 WM AND 80 WM

| Number of workers | Rel gain 40WM | Rel gain 80WM |
|---|---|---|
| 2 | 44.2% | 45.7% |
| 3 | 55.8% | 56.0% |
| 4 | 60.0% | 59.0% |
| 5 | 60.8% | 61.2% |
| 6 | 62.5% | 62.5% |

Table V also shows similar results for a configuration of 80 windmills. A large reduction in total maintenance time when a second worker is added, with a relative trade-off at 4 workers. The same results can be extrapolated to the use case of Taylormade products, since results are based on randomly chosen maintenance times, and the location of windmills and customers does not influence the final results of the JSSP.

### D. Combined results and Comparison

In order to determine the link between the optimal route resulting from solving VRPTW and the routes determined by solving the JSSP to minimize the time span of all maintenance jobs, a Pareto front is calculated. To compute this Pareto front with non-dominated solutions, tests were run on the two separate problems, and each result was then offered to the other problem. To clarify this, the following example is described: the ACO algorithm, VRPy and OR Tools solution methods ran to solve the VRPTW resulted in maintenance sequences with minimal total traveling distance. For this windmill sequence, the corresponding total time span for all maintenance tasks are calculated by adding the maintenance time for all jobs in this sequence. On the other hand, the total distances are computed for the sequences resulted from solving the JSSP (with minimal time span). This is done for sequences of 40 windmills and 3 vessels. Figure 4 shows the Pareto front.

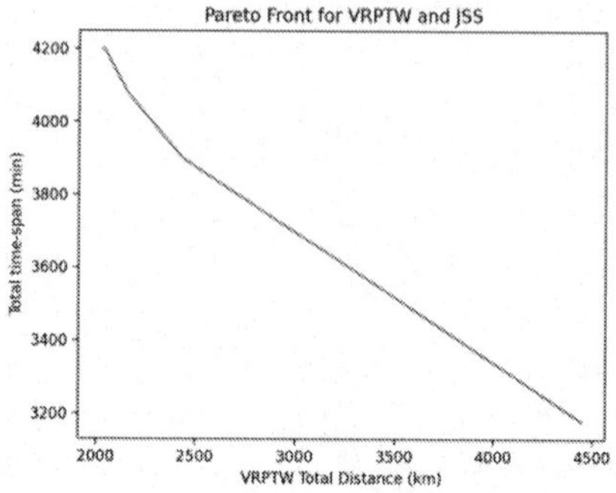


Figure 4. Pareto front for VRPTW-JSS comparison.

Our research has led to a group of Pareto optimal maintenance sequences as a result of the multi-objective optimization model (see coordinates in Table VI). However, it has proven to be very difficult to find a maintenance sequence that is optimal for both objectives. For example, the first and second jobs to be carried out initially according to minimize the total time span can be far away from each other, resulting in a total distance higher than the one obtained by solving the VRPTW. The tests resulted in maintenance paths that either have a low total time span and a high distance, or have a low distance but a high maintenance time span. In determining the optimal sequence, the planner has to decide which parameter is most important when making the choice. From all studied maintenance sequences, a list of 4 non-dominated solutions is obtained. Three of the solutions offer a path with a lower distance and a higher maintenance time span, one is showing a large distance and a lower time span. None of the tests resulted in a path with low values for both objectives.

TABLE VI
PARETO POINTS

| Coordinates | Distance VRPTW (min) | Distance JSSP (min) |
|---|---|---|
| 1 | 2156 | 4080 |
| 2 | 2436 | 3900 |
| 3 | 2037 | 4200 |
| 4 | 4444 | 3180 |

To compare the financial gain obtained by applying VRPTW and JSSP, we consider the case of 40 windmills and 3 workers.

- When reducing the distance from 8380km to 2064km with VRPTW, the financial gain is around 6180€. Fuel consumption is calculated as the distance traveled, multiplied by the weight of the vessel (30 tons), divided by 1000. The speed of the vessel is set at 5.5 km per hour, the fuel price is 2€ per liter, and no wind or current is taken into account.

- When setting the cost per hour downtime at 203€ and, from Table V, the reduction of the downtime at 67h, the total financial gain is 13600€.

The JSSP method thus leads to a much greater benefit than the distance reduction of the VRPTW solution.

## VI. Discussion | Evaluation

Of all methods tested to solve VRPTW, the OR Tools solver offers the quickest solutions, while VRPy and ACO generate similar results but much slower. Both use cases - windmill maintenance and product installation - show similar results with respect to the outcome of the solution method used and the calculation time needed. Also, for the JSSP, the OR Tools solver has proven to be fast and accurate. Comparing the solutions for both objective functions, being distance minimization and maintenance time span optimization, led to sequences that are only optimal for one of the two objectives. Therefore, Pareto points are calculated to obtain solutions that are as optimal as possible for both objectives. The planner can then use these resulting sequences to schedule maintenance tasks for a windmill park to minimize the distance traveled, downtime, or both. In all cases, this leads to a significant reduction in maintenance costs by reducing the fuel used or the loss of energy production. However, several constraints were not taken into account when solving VRPTW, such as sea currents, wind, and the capacity of the vessel. These can be integrated in future work to determine the impact they could have on the final results.

## VII. Conclusion and Future Work

When adding constraints to the VRP in the form of time windows for every windmill in which maintenance was needed, the relative gain obtained is 77% for a set of 40 windmills and 17% for a group of 8 windmills, spread over 3 farms, and this for all VRPTW solution methods used. Similar results were found and the same conclusions can be drawn for the second use case, the installation and maintenance of discrete products, showing the general applicability of all methods used to solve the VRPTW. A relative gain of the total maintenance span of almost 62.5% compared to the situation where all maintenance was done by one worker for a configuration with 40 windmills and 39% for 8 windmills was obtained when solving the JSSP. The total time needed for every added worker resulted in a higher total number of working hours to be paid. However, the total maintenance time span was more than halved, resulting in a significant gain in up-time.

In future research, other methods for solving VRPTW and JSSP can be studied and benchmarked. Possible other modi operandi to solve the VRPTW are (nonexhaustive): Harmony Search Algorithms (HAS), Memetic algorithms (MA), Genetic Algorithms (GA), the Hexaly solver, etc. For calculating the JSSP, heuristics or metaheuristics - such as Simulated Annealing, Tabu Search, ACO and Genetic Algorithms - can be compared. In addition, extended and different data sets can be investigated to further determine the applicability of the methods discussed.

## Acknowledgement

This work was executed within the project OPAL, Offshore Predictable Accessibility by Learning from data and experts with reference HBC.2020.3227, and funded by the Flemish government.

## References

[1] D. Fan et al., "A hybrid heuristic optimization of maintenance routing and scheduling for offshore wind farms", *Journal of Loss Prevention in the Process Industries*, vol. 62, 2019.

[2] R. Dawid, D. McMillan, and M. Revie, "Decision Support Tool for Offshore Wind Farm Vessel Routing under Uncertainty", *Energies*, vol. 11, 2018.

[3] D. Juliandri, H. Mawengkang, and F. Bu'ulolo, "Discrete Optimization Model for Vehicle Routing Problem with Scheduling Side Constraints", *IOP Conference Series: Materials Science and Engineering*, vol. 300, 2018.

[4] Z. Y. Zhang, "Multi-ACO Application in Routing and Scheduling Optimization of Maintenance Fleet (RSOMF) Based on Conditions for Offshore Wind Farms", *Journal of Power and Energy Engineering*, vol. 6, pp. 20–40, 2018.

[5] G. Laporte, "Fifty years of vehicle routing", *Transportation Science*, vol. 43, pp. 408–416, 2009.

[6] P. Toth and D. Vigo, "The vehicle routing problem", *Society for Industrial and Applied Mathematics*, vol. 107, pp. 32–42, 2002.

[7] N. A. El-Sherbeny, "Vehicle routing with time windows: An overview of exact, heuristic and metaheuristic methods", *Journal of King Saud University - Science*, vol. 22, pp. 123–131, 2010.

[8] R. Goel and R. Maini, "Vehicle routing problem and its solution methodologies: A survey", *Int. J. Logistics Systems and Management*, vol. 28, pp. 419–435, 2017.

[9] K. Braekers, K. Ramaekers, and I. Van Nieuwenhuyse, "The Vehicle Routing Problem: State of the Art Classification and Review", *Computers & Industrial Engineering*, vol. 99, 2015.

[10] D. G. N. D. Jayarathna, G. H. J. Lanel, and Z. A. M. S. Juman, "Industrial vehicle routing problem: a case study", *Journal of Shipping and Trade*, vol. 7, 2022.

[11] Google OR-Tools, "Vehicle Routing Problem with Time Windows", *https://developers.google.com/optimization/routing/vrptw*, 2022.

[12] F. Arnold, M. Gendreau, and K. Sörensen, "Efficiently solving very large-scale routing problems", *Computers and Operations Research*, vol. 107, pp. 32–42, 2019.

[13] J. Teunissen, "Improving production planning by flow shop scheduling algorithms : A case study at forfarmers", M.S. thesis, University of Twente, 2018.

[14] K. Bülbül and P. Kaminsky, "A Linear Programming-Based Method for Job Shop Scheduling", *Journal of Scheduling*, vol. 16, pp. 161–183, 2013.

[15] Y. Yu, "A Research Review on Job Shop Scheduling Problem", *E3S Web of Conferences*, vol. 253, 2021.

[16] A. Al-Shayea, E. Fararah, E. A. Nasr, and H. A. Mahmoud, "Model for Integrating Production Scheduling and Maintenance Planning of Flow Shop Production System", *Procedia Engineering*, vol. 8, pp. 208 826–208 835, 2020.

[17] R. Montagné and D. Torres Sanchez, "VRPy Documentation", *https://vrpy.readthedocs.io/en/latest/*, 2020.

[18] B. Catay, "Ant Colony Optimization and Its Application to the Vehicle Routing Problem with Pickups and Deliveries", *Natural Intelligence for Scheduling, Planning and Packing Problems. Studies in Computational Intelligence*, vol. 250, 2009.

[19] M. Dorigo, M. Birattari, and T. Stutzle, "Ant colony optimization", *IEEE Computational Intelligence Magazine*, vol. 1, pp. 28–39, 2006.

# Achievement of Collision Avoidance and Formation for Nonlinear Multi-Ship Systems Using an Interval Type-2 Fuzzy Tracking Approach

Wen-Jer Chang*
Department of Marine Engineering
National Taiwan Ocean University
Keelung, Taiwan, R.O.C.
email: wjchang@mail.ntou.edu.tw

Yann-Horng Lin
Department of Marine Engineering
National Taiwan Ocean University
Keelung, Taiwan, R.O.C.
email: ginobili9815318@gmail.com

***Abstract*—This paper addresses the challenges of formation and collision avoidance for Nonlinear Multi-Ship Systems (NM-ASs) using an Interval Type-2 (IT-2) fuzzy tracking controller. Since its significant value in military applications, the control of Multi-Agent Systems (M-ASs) has garnered considerable attention. To allocate tasks more properly within M-ASs, the leader-follower control scheme has been developed. However, the nonlinearities and uncertainties in ship dynamics continue to hinder task execution effectiveness. Compared to Type-1 Takagi-Sugeno Fuzzy Models (T-SFMs), IT-2 fuzzy control offers superior uncertainty handling and provides more precise control for NM-ASs. Previous research has introduced an IT-2 Formation-and-Containment (F-and-C) fuzzy control approach for multiple ships and combined some performance constraints to enhance the control efficiency of the leaders. Nonetheless, the safety of the leader ships, who are the most critical components of whole system, remains a concern until they can avoid obstacles and other ships. In this research, the Artificial Potential Fields (APFs) based-collision avoidance control is integrated with the IT-2 fuzzy control theory. Based on the IT-2 T-SFM, a fuzzy tracking control approach is developed to simultaneously achieve both collision avoidance and formation tasks. Finally, simulation results for four leader ships are presented to verify the efficiency and applicability of the proposed IT-2 fuzzy tracking controller.**

***Keywords-nonlinear multi-agent system; interval Type-2 fuzzy control; formation; tracking control; collision avoidance.***

## I. INTRODUCTION

Ships have long been essential in meeting the demands of both civilian and military sectors [1]. However, as the number of ships on the ocean continues to increase, safety concerns have become increasingly pressing. To address the issue, it is crucial not only to improve course management but also to ensure precise control over ship dynamics [2]. In practice, nonlinearities in ship dynamics arise from the complex marine environment [3], which makes designing controllers to ensure precise performance even more challenging. Moreover, the situation is compounded by uncertainties caused by equipment aging, rust, corrosion, biofouling, and other factors [4]. These issues further degrade the control performance of ships. In the past, the Takagi-Sugeno Fuzzy Model (T-SFM) has proven to be a powerful tool for the control and analysis of nonlinear systems. To overcome the limitations of the Type-1 T-SFM, the Interval Type-2 (IT-2) T-SFM has been introduced to better handle uncertainties [5]. In a complementary way, the Imperfect Premise Matching (IPM) fuzzy controller design has been systematically proposed in [5] to enable a more relaxed analysis process.

Unlike traditional applications, an increasing body of research has focused on deploying multiple unmanned vehicles to accomplish complex tasks [6]. With an appropriate cooperative topology among all units, the entire system can achieve common objectives more efficiently and effectively [7]. Consequently, control issues of Multi-Agent Systems (M-ASs) have garnered substantial attention from both academia and industry [8]. In the various objectives of M-ASs, Formation-and-Containment (F-and-C) controls remain two key topics that continue to be actively researched [9-10]. Formation control has seen significant development due to its broad applicability across diverse fields. However, nonlinearities and uncertainties in M-ASs often have a more pronounced impact than in single-agent systems. Building upon the T-SFM, many researchers have applied fuzzy control methods to complete formation or containment objectives [11-12]. Additionally, some researchers have tackled the F-and-C problems simultaneously using the T-SFM [13]. Nevertheless, the limitations of Type-1 T-SFM in managing uncertain factors can undermine the effectiveness of Nonlinear M-ASs (NM-ASs). These uncertainties can lead to imprecise system dynamics, with errors propagating sequentially one after another, ultimately causing collisions and system failure.

However, the F-and-C control based on the IT-2 T-SFM remains an open issue. Some researchers have successfully developed IT-2 fuzzy containment control approaches [14]. Nevertheless, these studies considered the leaders as open-loop systems. From a practical application perspective, it is essential to ensure the stability of the leaders as well. If the leaders are unstable, the followers will also become unstable, even if they are contained within the region formed by the leaders [13-14]. Recently, our research proposed an IT-2 fuzzy control approach to achieve F-and-C [15]. In this control problem, leader crashes can significantly impact the entire NM-AS and may even result in its collapse. To further ensure the reliability of leaders, anti-disturbance capabilities were also incorporated. However, the safety of the leaders remains uncertain unless they can actively avoid other ships or obstacles. In recent decades, collision avoidance control based on the Artificial Potential Field (APF) method has been widely adopted for its intuitive nature and ease of implementation [16]. The APF approach has proven to be an effective solution for collision avoidance due to the reduction of computational time. This advantage has also demonstrated the suitability of the APF method for application in scenarios involving multiple-ship encounters [17]. Therefore, the APF is combined with the IT-2 fuzzy tracking controller design in this research to achieve both collision avoidance and formation for leader ships.

The organization of this research is provided as follows. In Section II, the nonlinear system and the IT-2 T-SFM are presented for the leaders in NM-AS. In Section III, an IT-2 fuzzy controller design approach in terms of the IPM concept is proposed for the achievement of collision avoidance and formation. In Section IV, the simulation results are given for four leader ships. In Section V, some conclusions and future works are given for this research.

## II. NM-AS AND IT-2 T-SFM

A nonlinear system is presented to describe the dynamic behaviors of NM-AS by extending the mathematical model in [18] in this section. Taking into account the effects of uncertain factors, the IT-2 T-SFM is also built. First, the NM-AS is considered as follows.

$$\dot{x}_1^\varepsilon(t) = \vartheta^\varepsilon(t)x_4^\varepsilon(t) - \phi^\varepsilon(t)x_5^\varepsilon(t) \tag{1}$$

$$\dot{x}_2^\varepsilon(t) = \phi^\varepsilon(t)x_4^\varepsilon(t) + \vartheta^\varepsilon(t)x_5^\varepsilon(t) \tag{2}$$

$$\dot{x}_3^\varepsilon(t) = \varphi^\varepsilon(t)x_6^\varepsilon(t) \tag{3}$$

$$\dot{x}_4^\varepsilon(t) = -0.0318x_4^\varepsilon(t) + 0.8870u_1^\varepsilon(t) \tag{4}$$

$$\dot{x}_5^\varepsilon(t) = -0.0628x_5^\varepsilon(t) - 0.0030x_6^\varepsilon(t) + 0.5415u_2^\varepsilon(t) + 0.3152u_3^\varepsilon(t) \tag{5}$$

$$\dot{x}_6^\varepsilon(t) = -0.0045x_5^\varepsilon(t) - 0.2427x_6^\varepsilon(t) + 0.3152u_2^\varepsilon(t) + 8.0082u_3^\varepsilon(t) \tag{6}$$

where $\varphi^\varepsilon(t) = 1 + \Delta^\varepsilon(t)$, $\vartheta^\varepsilon(t) = cos(x_3^\varepsilon(t)) + \Delta^\varepsilon(t)$, $\phi^\varepsilon(t) = sin(x_3^\varepsilon(t)) + \Delta^\varepsilon(t)$, $x_1^\varepsilon(t)$, $x_2^\varepsilon(t)$ and $x_3^\varepsilon(t)$ are the $(x, y)$ position and yaw angle on earth-fixed coordinate, $x_4^\varepsilon(t)$, $x_5^\varepsilon(t)$ and $x_6^\varepsilon(t)$ are the velocities of surge motion, sway motion and the yaw angle variation, $u_1^\varepsilon(t)$, $u_2^\varepsilon(t)$ and $u_3^\varepsilon(t)$ are the forces and moments generated by thrusters, $\Delta^\varepsilon(t)$ are the uncertain factors, each leader is indexed with the number $\varepsilon = 1,2,3,4$. In this research, the different situations of uncertainties, $\Delta^{1,2}(t) = 0.1cos(t)$ and $\Delta^{3,4}(t) = 0.1sin(t)$, are considered for four leaders.

To make the control problem clearer, Fig. 1 is presented for four leaders with the four target trajectories and two obstacles.

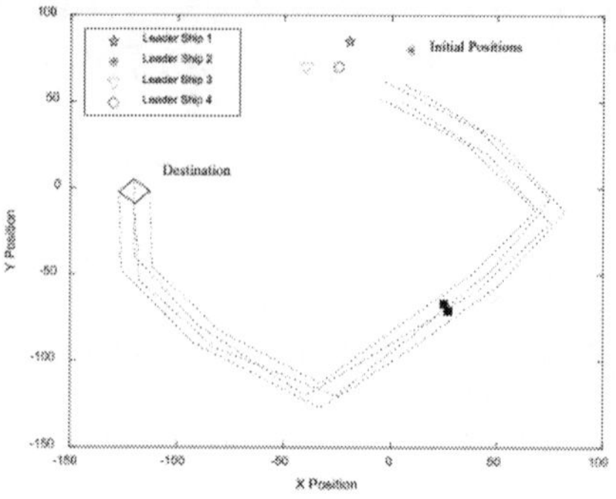


Figure 1. Formation and collision avoidance problems.

According to Fig. 1, the formation objective of the four leader ships is to track the trajectory and maintain the rectangular formation until reaching the destination on the left-hand side. It is assumed that there is an uncrossable obstacle between the initial positions of the four leaders and the destination. Within the target trajectories, two obstacles need to be avoided.

*Remark 1*

Based on the findings in [15], the individual tracking controller for each leader can efficiently accomplish the formation task and define the dynamics of the entire system. Furthermore, communication between the leaders that are farthest apart from each other is not required. In this research, only the formation problem of the leaders in [15] is considered, so the communication topology is not necessary.

Covering the uncertain factors in the representation, the IT-2 T-SFM is constructed for the NM-AS (1)-(6) as follows.

$$\dot{x}^\varepsilon(t) = \sum_{\alpha=1}^{3} \tilde{\Omega}_\alpha(x_3^\varepsilon(t))\{\mathbf{A}_\alpha x^\varepsilon(t) + \mathbf{B}_\alpha u^\varepsilon(t)\} \tag{7}$$

where $u^\varepsilon(t) = [u_1^\varepsilon(t) \;\; u_2^\varepsilon(t) \;\; u_3^\varepsilon(t)]^T$, $x^\varepsilon(t) = [x_1^\varepsilon(t) \;\; x_2^\varepsilon(t) \;\; x_3^\varepsilon(t) \;\; x_4^\varepsilon(t) \;\; x_5^\varepsilon(t) \;\; x_6^\varepsilon(t)]^T$. To save space, the model matrices in (7) are referred to [15] and will not be presented. The upper and lower bound membership functions are designed as follows.

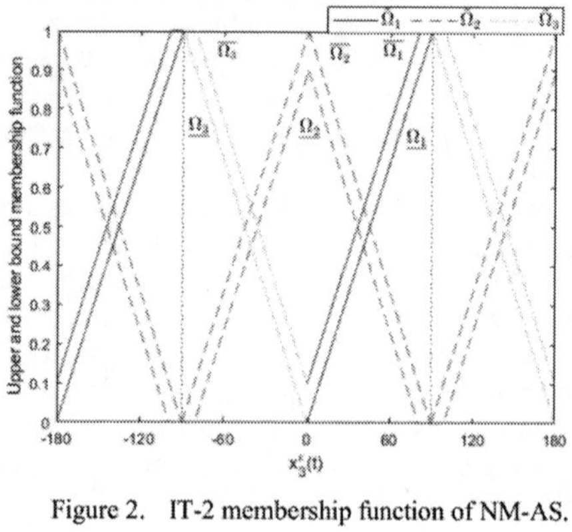


Figure 2. IT-2 membership function of NM-AS.

*Remark 2*

It is worth noting that nearly all T-SFMs in the existing literature are established for an operating range between -90° and 90°. However, the desired yaw angle, obtained through the APF for collision avoidance, may fall outside this range. This could lead to instability of the ships, as the desired yaw angle must be tracked. To address this issue, the membership functions originally defined for the ranges from 0° to 90° and -90° to 0° are extended to cover the ranges from -180° to -90° and 90° to 180°, as shown in Fig. 2.

According to [5] and the IT-2 membership function of Fig. 2, the firing strength can be obtained as follows.

$$\boldsymbol{\Omega}_\alpha\left(x_3^\varepsilon(t)\right)=\left[\underline{\Omega}_\alpha\left(x_3^\varepsilon(t)\right),\bar{\Omega}_\alpha\left(x_3^\varepsilon(t)\right)\right] \quad (8)$$

where upper bound and lower bound membership functions of (8) are denoted as Fig. 2. Then, the following calculation can be obtained for the IT-2 T-SFM.

$$\tilde{\Omega}_\alpha\left(x_3^\varepsilon(t)\right)=\bar{\tau}_\alpha\left(x_3^\varepsilon(t)\right)\bar{\Omega}_\alpha\left(x_3^\varepsilon(t)\right)+\underline{\tau}_\alpha\left(x_3^\varepsilon(t)\right)\underline{\Omega}_\alpha\left(x_3^\varepsilon(t)\right) \quad (9)$$

where $\bar{\tau}_\alpha\left(x_3^\varepsilon(t)\right)$ and $\underline{\tau}_\alpha\left(x_3^\varepsilon(t)\right)$ are the functions associated with uncertainties and not necessary to be known. As the membership functions, these functions satisfy the conditions $\bar{\tau}_\alpha\left(x_3^\varepsilon(t)\right)+\underline{\tau}_\alpha\left(x_3^\varepsilon(t)\right)=1$ and $1\geq\bar{\tau}_\alpha\left(x_3^\varepsilon(t)\right)\geq\underline{\tau}_\alpha\left(x_3^\varepsilon(t)\right)\geq 0$.

Referring to (7), the following IT-2 T-SFM is also constructed for IT-2 fuzzy tracking approach to achieve the formation and collision avoidance purposes.

$${}^m\dot{x}_d^\varepsilon(t)=\sum_{\alpha=1}^{3}\tilde{\Omega}_\alpha\left(x_3^\varepsilon(t)\right)\left\{\mathbf{A}_\alpha\,{}^m x_d^\varepsilon(t)\right\} \quad (10)$$

where ${}^m x_d^\varepsilon(t)$ is the desired system states to be tracked, $m=c,f$ denotes the collision avoidance mode and formation mode of leader ships.

Subtracting the T-SFM (10) from (7), the error dynamic system can be obtained as follows.

$${}^m\dot{e}^\varepsilon(t)=\sum_{\alpha=1}^{3}\tilde{\Omega}_\alpha\left(x_3^\varepsilon(t)\right)\left\{\mathbf{A}_\alpha\,{}^m e^\varepsilon(t)+\mathbf{B}_\alpha\,{}^m u^\varepsilon(t)\right\} \quad (11)$$

where ${}^m e^\varepsilon(t)={}^m x^\varepsilon(t)-{}^m x_d^\varepsilon(t)$.

According to the IT-2 T-SFM (11), a fuzzy tracking controller design approach is proposed to simultaneously achieve the collision avoidance and formation for leaders.

## III. IT-2 Fuzzy Collision Avoidance and Formation Controller Design

In this section, the IT-2 fuzzy controller design and stability analysis are proposed based on the IPM concept for leader ships in NM-AS (1)-(6). Moreover, the information of IT-2 membership function, which is more flexible than Type-1 membership function, is combined into the stability condition to reduce the conservativeness. According to the IPM concept in [5] and T-SFM (11), the IT-2 fuzzy tracking controller is proposed as follows.

$${}^m u^\varepsilon(t)=\sum_{\beta=1}^{2}\Gamma_\beta\left(x_3^\varepsilon(t)\right)\left\{\mathbf{F}_\beta\,{}^m e^\varepsilon(t)\right\} \quad (12)$$

where $\mathbf{F}_\beta$ are the feedback gains to be designed for the tracking purpose. The IT-2 membership function for the fuzzy controller (12) is designed as follows.

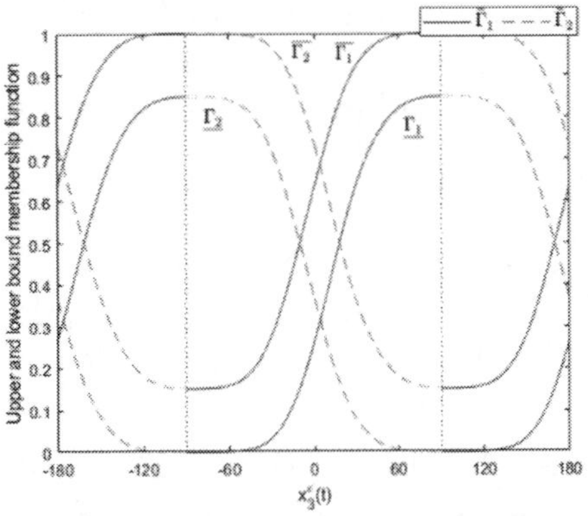


Figure 3. IT-2 membership function of fuzzy controller.

Note that one of the advantages of the IPM approach is that the form of the membership function and the number of rules can be designed differently from those in the T-S fuzzy model. Similar to the process (8)-(9), the firing strength of fuzzy controller (12) can be defined as follows.

$$\boldsymbol{\Gamma}_\alpha\left(x_3^\varepsilon(t)\right)=\left[\underline{\Gamma}_\alpha\left(x_3^\varepsilon(t)\right),\bar{\Gamma}_\alpha\left(x_3^\varepsilon(t)\right)\right] \quad (13)$$

where upper and lower bound membership functions are presented in Fig. 3. For the fuzzy controller (12), the IT-2 membership function is given as follows.

$$\tilde{\Gamma}_\alpha\left(x_3^\varepsilon(t)\right)=\bar{\gamma}_\alpha\left(x_3^\varepsilon(t)\right)\bar{\Gamma}_\alpha\left(x_3^\varepsilon(t)\right)+\underline{\gamma}_\alpha\left(x_3^\varepsilon(t)\right)\underline{\Gamma}_\alpha\left(x_3^\varepsilon(t)\right) \quad (14)$$

where $\bar{\gamma}_\alpha\left(x_3^\varepsilon(t)\right)$ and $\underline{\gamma}_\alpha\left(x_3^\varepsilon(t)\right)$ are the functions satisfy same conditions as $\bar{\tau}_\alpha\left(x_3^\varepsilon(t)\right)$ and $\underline{\tau}_\alpha\left(x_3^\varepsilon(t)\right)$. The functions are predefined since the fuzzy controller is designed by users.

Substituting the IT-2 fuzzy tracking controller (12) into the T-SFM (11), the following closed-loop model is derived.

$$ {}^{m}\dot{e}(t)=\sum_{\alpha=1}^{3}\sum_{\beta=1}^{2}\tilde{\Xi}_{\alpha\beta}\left(x_3(t)\right)\left\{\left(\mathbf{I}\otimes\left(\mathbf{A}_\alpha+\mathbf{B}_\alpha\mathbf{F}_\beta\right)\right){}^{m}e(t)\right\} \quad (15) $$

where $\tilde{\Xi}_{\alpha\beta}\left(x_3(t)\right)=\tilde{\Omega}_\alpha\left(x_3(t)\right)\tilde{\Gamma}_\beta\left(x_3(t)\right)$ and $\otimes$ is the Kronecker product.

Note that according to [15], the stability analysis process needs to be developed only for one leader ship in (15). Referring to [5], the stability criterion for the tracking purpose is obtained as follows.

*Theorem 1*

Given the scalars $\bar{\sigma}_{\alpha\beta i_3}$ and $\underline{\sigma}_{\alpha\beta i_3}$, if there exist the positive definite matrices $\mathbf{Q}$, $\mathbf{N}_{\alpha\beta}$ and the symmetric matrix $\mathbf{M}$ such that the following sufficient conditions are all satisfied, the tracking purpose for the collision avoidance and formation can be achieved for leader ships.

$$ \sum_{\alpha=1}^{3}\sum_{\beta=1}^{2}\left(\underline{\sigma}_{\alpha\beta i_3}\mathbf{\Phi}_{\alpha\beta}-\left(\underline{\sigma}_{\alpha\beta i_3}-\bar{\sigma}_{\alpha\beta i_3}\right)\mathbf{N}_{\alpha\beta}+\underline{\sigma}_{\alpha\beta i_3}\mathbf{M}\right)-\mathbf{M}<0 $$

$$ \text{for all } i_3=1,2 \quad (16) $$

$$ \mathbf{\Phi}_{\alpha\beta}-\mathbf{N}_{\alpha\beta}+\mathbf{M}<0 \quad \text{for all } \alpha,\beta \quad (17) $$

where $\mathbf{\Phi}_{\alpha\beta}=\mathbf{A}_\alpha\mathbf{Q}+\mathbf{B}_\alpha\mathbf{G}_\beta+\mathbf{Q}\mathbf{A}_\alpha^{\mathrm{T}}+\mathbf{G}_\beta^{\mathrm{T}}\mathbf{B}_\alpha^{\mathrm{T}}$, $\mathbf{G}_\beta=\mathbf{F}_\beta\mathbf{Q}$, $\mathbf{Q}=\mathbf{P}^{-1}$. Note that $\bar{\sigma}_{\alpha\beta i_3}$, $\underline{\sigma}_{\alpha\beta i_3}$ and $i_3$ are the parameters related to the IT-2 membership function in Figs. 2-3. To save the place, the derivation process will not be provided and it can refer to [5] and [15].

After the IT-2 fuzzy tracking controller is designed by Theorem 1, the purpose of formation and collision avoidance can be determined by the following process.

First, the desired system state to be tracked in the formation mode is designed as follows.

$$ {}^{f}e^{\varepsilon}(t)=\left[{}^{f}e_1^{\varepsilon}(t)\quad {}^{f}e_2^{\varepsilon}(t)\quad {}^{f}e_3^{\varepsilon}(t)\quad x_4^{\varepsilon}(t)\quad x_5^{\varepsilon}(t)\quad x_6^{\varepsilon}(t)\right]^{\mathrm{T}} \quad (18) $$

In this research, the tracking purpose is focused on the first three states. This is because the first two states directly specify the ships' positions, and the third state ensures the correction of the ships' course. As extended from Remark 2, most of the existing literature deals primarily with the stability of ships, which means that the yaw angle must track solely the zero value. However, the T-SFM-based fuzzy controller design methods cannot be applied to this research due to the operating range limitations.

Note that the desired x and y positions are obtained using a first-order hold between two positions. Moreover, the desired yaw angle is also derived from these two positions.

Then, the purpose of collision avoidance mode is ensured by the desired system states as follows.

$$ {}^{c}e^{\varepsilon}(t)=\left[{}^{c}e_1^{\varepsilon}(t)\quad {}^{c}e_2^{\varepsilon}(t)\quad {}^{c}e_3^{\varepsilon}(t)\quad x_4^{\varepsilon}(t)\quad x_5^{\varepsilon}(t)\quad x_6^{\varepsilon}(t)\right]^{\mathrm{T}} \quad (19) $$

Building on the results in [17] and [19], the desired yaw angle can be derived from the combination of the source and vortex fields of the APF approach for collision avoidance. First, the gradient of vortex velocity field is given as follows.

$$ \nabla\Theta_v=\left(v_{xv},v_{yv}\right)=\left(-\frac{y_s(t)-y_a(t)}{r^2},\frac{x_s(t)-x_a(t)}{r^2}\right) \quad (20) $$

where $x_a$, $y_a$ are the $(x,y)$ positions of ships to be avoided and $x_o$, $y_o$ are the $(x,y)$ positions of ship itself. In addition, the gradient of source velocity field is given as follows.

$$ \nabla\Theta_s=\left(v_{xs},v_{ys}\right)=\left(v_r cos\theta+v_\theta sin\theta, v_r sin\theta+v_\theta cos\theta\right) \quad (21) $$

where $v_r=\frac{1}{r}$ and $v_\theta=0$. Note that for both vortex and source potential fields, the radius and angle are derived by the following process.

$$ {}_{p}r=\sqrt{\left(x_s(t)-{}_{p}x_a(t)\right)^2+\left(y_s(t)-{}_{p}y_a(t)\right)^2} \quad (22) $$

$$ {}_{p}\theta=tan^{-1}\left(\left(y_s(t)-{}_{p}y_a(t)\right)/\left(x_s(t)-{}_{p}x_a(t)\right)\right) \quad (23) $$

where $p$ is the number of ships to be avoided in multiple ship encounter scenario. Then, the desired yaw angle for ship to avoid the collision is derived as follows for both vortex and source fields.

$$ \psi_d=tan^{-1}\left(v_{yv}/v_{xv}\right) \quad \text{or} \quad tan^{-1}\left(v_{ys}/v_{xs}\right) \quad (24) $$

However, the $x$ and $y$ positions are also required to be tracked in this research. Therefore, the desired positions are also derived from desired yaw angle, which is obtained by APF approach (20)-(24), as follows.

$$ x_{1d}(t)=x_s(t)+Lcos(\psi_d) \quad (25) $$

$$ x_{2d}(t)=y_s(t)+Lsin(\psi_d) \quad (26) $$

where $L$ is the distance between the desired point and the ships' own point. In the combination of the two APFs, the vortex field is used to change the ship's course for collision avoidance, while the source field generates a repulsive course to prevent the ship from getting too close to obstacles. To determine when to use which APF, the following condition is provided.

*Condition 1*

If $R_s < r \le R_v$, then $\psi_d = tan^{-1}\left(\dfrac{v_{yv}}{v_{xv}}\right)$.

If $0 < r \le R_s$, then $\psi_d = tan^{-1}\left(\dfrac{v_{ys}}{v_{xs}}\right)$.

where $R_v$ and $R_s$ are the triggered distance of vortex and source velocity field. Moreover, the following condition is also given for the determination of tracking and avoidance mode by referring to [17].

*Condition 2*

If $DCPA \le R_f$ and TCPA > 0, then $\psi_d = tan^{-1}\left(v_{yv}/v_{xv}\right)$; otherwise, $\psi_d = x_{3d}^{c}(t)$, where $R_f$ is the safe collision range of leader ships.

In the next section, the simulation results with four leader ships are presented to demonstrate the effectiveness and applicability of the designed IT-2 fuzzy controller.

## IV. SIMULATION OF NM-AS

With the vortex and source velocity APFs, the collision avoidance approach for multiple ships is proposed with an IT-2 fuzzy tracking controller design. First, the control gains are obtained as follows by solving the control problem in Theorem 1 using MATLAB.

$$\mathbf{F}_1 = \begin{bmatrix} -0.6013 & -0.4007 & -0.0101 & -2.4117 & -0.2879 & -0.0029 \\ 0.7777 & -0.6088 & 0.0346 & 0.5683 & -2.6147 & 0.0690 \\ -0.0311 & 0.0050 & -0.4411 & -0.0231 & 0.0359 & -0.8179 \end{bmatrix} \tag{27}$$

$$\mathbf{F}_2 = \begin{bmatrix} -0.6269 & 0.3987 & 0.0101 & -2.5153 & 0.2857 & 0.0029 \\ -0.7723 & -0.6624 & 0.0381 & -0.5650 & -2.8564 & 0.0770 \\ 0.0309 & 0.0077 & -0.4563 & 0.0229 & 0.0493 & -0.8580 \end{bmatrix} \tag{28}$$

According to Remark 2, the following control gains can be derived for the case of -180° to -90° and 90° to 180°.

$$\mathbf{F}_1 = \begin{bmatrix} 0.6013 & 0.4007 & -0.0101 & -2.4117 & -0.2879 & -0.0029 \\ -0.7777 & 0.6088 & 0.0346 & 0.5683 & -2.6147 & 0.0690 \\ 0.0311 & -0.0050 & -0.4411 & -0.0231 & 0.0359 & -0.8179 \end{bmatrix} \tag{29}$$

$$\mathbf{F}_2 = \begin{bmatrix} 0.6269 & -0.3987 & 0.0101 & -2.5153 & 0.2857 & 0.0029 \\ 0.7723 & 0.6624 & 0.0381 & -0.5650 & -2.8564 & 0.0770 \\ -0.0309 & -0.0077 & -0.4563 & 0.0229 & 0.0493 & -0.8580 \end{bmatrix} \tag{30}$$

To begin with the simulation, the ranges for collision avoidance mode are designed as follows.

$$R_f = 4 \ , \ R_v = 4 \ , \ R_s = 2 \ \text{and} \ L = 2 \tag{31}$$

Then, by applying the IT-2 fuzzy controller (12) with the gains (27)-(30) for different ranges, the simulation results are presented as follows based on the consideration of (31).

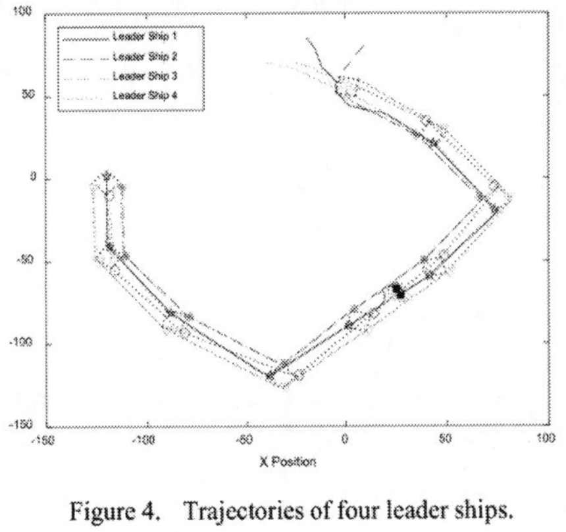


Figure 4. Trajectories of four leader ships.

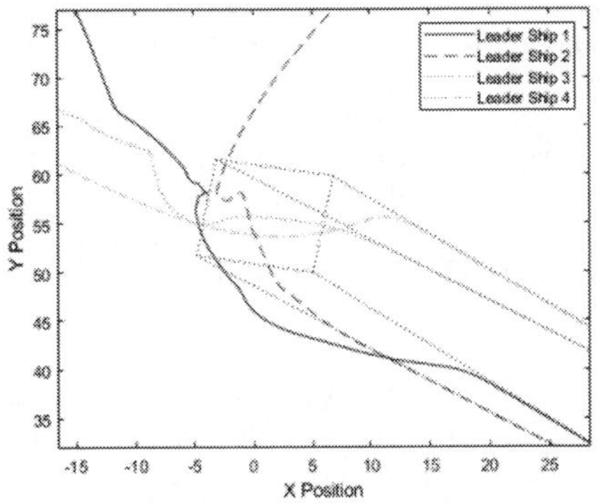


Figure 5. Trajectories of four leader ships in tracking situation.

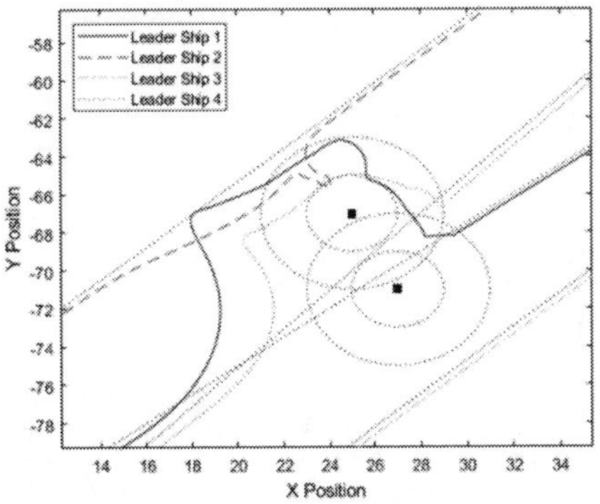


Figure 6. Trajectories of four leader ships in avoidance situation.

From Fig. 4, one can see that four leader ships successfully track the individual desired trajectory and thus form the rectangular region. Moreover, the region can be sustained until the destination is reached. In Fig. 5, the trajectories of the four ships before the first formation are presented. It is observed that the ships can efficiently avoid each other before tracking their desired trajectories. The vortex velocity APF turns the ships in the right direction, complying with the COLREGs as [17], and all ships move to the right when encountering others. More importantly, the four leader ships can simultaneously avoid two obstacles and each other when the obstacles are on their trajectories in Fig. 6. The outer and inner black dot circles denote the ranges of the triggering vortex and source APFs, respectively.

## V. CONCLUSIONS

An IT-2 fuzzy tracking controller design approach has been developed in this research to simultaneously meet the requirements of collision avoidance and formation control for multiple ships. Based on the IT-2 T-SFM, the dynamic behaviors of NM-ASs can be more completely described by accounting for the uncertain factors in the IT-2 membership function. According to the IPM concept, a more flexible fuzzy tracking controller design process can be developed. By combining vortex and source velocity APFs, the IT-2 fuzzy controller can achieve the avoidance objective. As stated in Conditions 1-2, all ships can properly switch between formation and collision avoidance modes. Based on the simulation results, the IT-2 fuzzy controller can efficiently accomplish both formation and collision avoidance tasks, even under multiple encounter scenarios. In the future, the fuzzy control theory can be considered to obtain the smoother adjustment between different modes. The containment purpose of follower ships can also be integrated into the IT-2 fuzzy controller design.

## ACKNOWLEDGMENT

This work was supported by the National Science and Technology Council of the Republic of China under Contract NSTC113-2221-E-019-032.

## REFERENCES

[1] Z. H. Munim, "Autonomous Ships: a Review, Innovative Applications and Future Maritime Business Models," Supply Chain Forum: An International Journal, vol. 20, pp. 266-279, Jun. 2019, doi: 10.1080/16258312.2019.1631714

[2] T. Perez, Ship Motion Control: Course Keeping and Roll Stabilisation Using Rudder and Fins, London: Springer-Verlag, 1st ed., 2005.

[3] S. D. Adlinge, P. D. Shendge, and D. D. Dhadekar, "Robust Control of Unmanned Sea Surface Vehicle Using Inertial Delay Control," Journal of Marine Science and Technology, vol. 29, pp. 556-599, Jul. 2024, doi:10.1007/s00773-024-01012-4.

[4] D. K. Jana, B. Bej, M. H. Abd Wahab, and A. Mukherjee, "Novel Type-2 Fuzzy Logic Approach for Inference of Corrosion Failure Likelihood of Oil and Gas Pipeline Industry," Engineering Failure Analysis, vol. 80, pp. 299-311, Oct. 2017, doi: 10.1016/j.engfailanal.2017.06.046.

[5] H. K. Lam, H. Li, C. Deters, E. L. Secco, H. A. Wurdemann, and K. Althoefer, "Control Design for Interval Type-2 Fuzzy Systems under Imperfect Premise Matching," IEEE Transactions on Industrial Electronics, vol. 61, pp. 956-968, Feb. 2014, doi: 10.1109/TIE.2013.2253064.

[6] G. Wu, T. Xu, Y. Sun, and J. Zhang, "Review of Multiple Unmanned Surface Vessels Collaborative Search and Hunting Based on Swarm Intelligence," International Journal of Advanced Robotic Systems, vol. 19, p. 17298806221091885, Apr. 2022, doi:10.1177/1729880622109188.

[7] W. Ren, R. W. Beard, and E. M. Atkins, "Information Consensus in Multivehicle Cooperative Control," IEEE Control Systems Magazine, vol. 27, pp. 71-82, Apr. 2007, doi:10.1109/MCS.2007.338264.

[8] V. Gorodetsky, P. Skobelev, and V. Marik, "System Engineering View on Multi-Agent Technology for Industrial Applications: Barriers and Prospects," Cybernetics and Physics, vol. 9, pp. 13-30, Jun. 2020, doi:10.35470/2226-4116-2020-9-1-13-30.

[9] Y. Liu, J. Liu, Z. He, Z. Li, Q. Zhang, and Z. Ding, "A Survey of Multi-Agent Systems on Distributed Formation Control," Unmanned Systems, vol. 12, pp. 913-926, May 2023, doi: 10.1142/S2301385024500274.

[10] H. Wang, H. Li, Y. Feng, and Y. Li, "Fixed-Time Coordinated Guidance for Containment Maneuvering of Unmanned Surface Vehicles under Delayed Communications: Theory and Experiment," Ocean Engineering, vol. 277, p. 114249, Jun. 2023, doi:10.1016/j.oceaneng.2023.114249.

[11] L. Feng, B. Huang, and X. Xie, "Dynamic Event-Triggered Containment Control for T–S Fuzzy Multiagent Systems With Actuator Faults," IEEE Systems Journal, vol. 18, pp. 1538-1548, Sep. 2024, doi:10.1109/JSYST.2024.3408607.

[12] W. Wang, C. Huang, H. K. Lam, and L. Wang, "Formation Control of TS Fuzzy Systems with Event-Triggered Sampling Scheme via Membership Function Dependent Approach," Information Sciences, vol. 622, pp. 842-858, Apr. 2023, doi:10.1016/j.ins.2022.11.110.

[13] Y. H. Lin, W. J. Chang, and C. L. Pen, "Fuzzy Steering Control for TS Fuzzy Model-Based Multiple Ship Systems Subject to Formation and Containment," International Journal of Fuzzy Systems, vol. 25, pp. 1782-1794, Mar. 2023, doi:10.1007/s40815-023-01479-0.

[14] S. Yan, H. Qian, P. Ding, S. Chu, and H. Wang, "Finite-Time Tolerant Containment Control for IT2 T–S Fuzzy Network Multi-Agent Systems with Actuator Faults, Packet Dropouts and DoS Attacks," ISA Transactions, vol. 137, pp. 199-209, Jun. 2023, doi:10.1016/j.isatra.2023.01.036.

[15] W. J. Chang, Y. H. Lin, Y. C. Lee, and C. C. Ku, "Investigating Formation and Containment Problem for Nonlinear Multi-Agent Systems via Interval Type-2 Fuzzy Sliding Mode Tracking Approach," IEEE Transactions on Fuzzy Systems, Jul. 2024, 10.1109/TFUZZ.2024.3387045.

[16] O. Khatib, "Real-Time Obstacle Avoidance for Manipulators and Mobile Robots," The International Journal of Robotics Research, vol. 5, pp. 90-98, Mar. 1986, doi:10.1177/027836498600500106.

[17] M. C. Lee, C. Y. Nieh, H. C. Kuo, and J. C. Huang, "A Collision Avoidance Method for Multi-Ship Encounter Situations," Journal of Marine Science and Technology, vol. 25, pp. 925-942, Nov. 2019, doi:10.1007/s00773-019-00691-8.

[18] T. I. Fossen, and A. Grovlen, "Nonlinear Output Feedback Control of Dynamically Positioned Ships Using Vectorial Observer Backstepping," IEEE Transactions on Control Systems Technology, vol. 6, pp. 121-128, Jan. 1998, doi:10.1109/87.654882.

[19] M. C. Lee, C. Y. Nieh, H. C. Kuo, and J. C. Huang, "An Automatic Collision Avoidance and Route Generating Algorithm for Ships Based on Field Model," Journal of Marine Science and Technology, vol. 27, pp. 101-113, Apr. 2021, doi:10.6119/JMST.201904_27(2).0003.

# Exploring the Role of User Experience in Enhancing IoT Applications for Smart Manufacturing: A Review

Leigh Johnston, Kyle Madden, Justin Quinn, Sonya Coleman, Dermot Kerr
SCEIS Cognitive Robotics Laboratory
Ulster University
Derry/Londonderry, Northern Ireland
e-mail: v.johnston@ulster.ac.uk, k.madden@ulster.ac.uk, jp.quinn@ulster.ac.uk, sa.coleman@ulster.ac.uk, d.kerr@ulster.ac.uk

*Abstract*—**The paper highlights the lack of a human-machine experience within Smart Manufacturing when using Internet of Things technologies, along with challenges, and provides recommendations for enhancement. The use of Internet of Things technologies in Smart Manufacturing has grown steadily since the launch of Industry 4.0 in 2011. Since then, the data collected from these technologies have assisted manufacturers in becoming digitally savvy by helping them gain a deeper understanding of their production processes, how they can become more efficient, and by revealing innovative ways to grow their business whilst remaining competitive. However, an area that needs further consideration is the user experience of these technologies and the human they are designed for. This paper critically examines current frameworks and methodologies that have been created to enhance the human-machine experience of Smart Manufacturing systems, some of which target the needs of industry, individual, or Internet of Things technologies. From this review, we identify that there is not one framework or methodology that can cater to the needs of all three. Additionally, open challenges that have been encountered are discussed, and suggestions for possible future directions are explored, these include focusing on human-centred design and the well-being of workers by adapting Internet of Things interfaces to the system's user needs within a Smart Manufacturing realm.**

***Keywords-Smart Manufacturing; Internet of Things; User Experience; Applications.***

## I. INTRODUCTION

The COVID-19 pandemic significantly affected sectors, such as tourism, hospitality, and aviation; however, it also had a major impact on manufacturing production lines and global supply chains, highlighting its vulnerability in areas including finance, organisation, and technology [1][2].

To navigate future pandemics, challenges, and uncertainties, businesses within the realm of manufacturing are investing in sustainable digital solutions to help future-proof their operations. According to the 2024 Material Handling Industry (MHI) Annual Industry Report in partnership with Deloitte, 85% of supply chain leaders are considering the implementation of Internet of Things (IoT) devices to their production lines within the next five years [3]. In addition, 75% are also considering the use of wearable and mobile technologies to augment operations [3]. If fulfilled, it is estimated that supply chain leaders could gain a 39% and 40% competitive advantage, respectively, over their competitors [3]. With the additional implementation of Artificial Intelligence (AI), supply chain leaders have the potential to disrupt the industry by 11% and potentially have a 40% competitive advantage [3]. Whilst these figures are promising, challenges remain in terms of a human-centred strategy, for example, the collaboration between the human workforce and automation according to 45% of supply chain leaders [3]. In the report 44% of leaders noted that one of the main reasons for incorporating such technologies is to enable better decision-making and visibility into data [3]. However, one of the top 5 challenges reported was a talent shortage [3]. John Paxton, the Chief Executive Officer (CEO) of MHI stated, "The focus on technology in supply chains is undeniable. But supply chains are run by people, and human-centricity is the key" [3].

Therefore, the User Experience (UX) of these technologies should be enhanced to work in conjunction with the employee by understanding and adapting to their needs, well-being, and intelligence regardless of their educational background or disabilities - UX relates to how a user interacts with an application [4]. In turn, this could produce a robust and empowering co-working experience between humans and machines, address the talent shortage and lack of a hum-centred strategy, and minimise the impact on business operations.

This paper utilised a hybrid methodology, comprising of a systematic and scoping review. A systematic structured approach with a predefined inclusion and exclusion criteria, and a scoping review to identify gaps within various formats of literature. The inclusion criteria are: a date range of 2019-2025; the scope of the review was within UX, industry, and augmented systems; the search terms consisted of augmented manufacturing, UX, and Industry 5.0; and the language of papers were to be in English. The exclusion criteria included: not within the predefined date range; not including the types of data defined or search terms; and not in the English language. The research questions are as follows:

*1) What frameworks and/or methodologies are currently being used to measure the UX of IoT technologies in Smart Manufacturing?*

*2) What challenges do the frameworks and methodologies present?*

*3) How can the UX of IoT technologies in Smart Manufacturing be enhanced?*

To address these aforementioned issues and utilise the methodology described to answer the research questions, the paper outline is as follows: Section 2 is an overview of UX in manufacturing, Section 3 details the background to IoT devices, Section 4 showcases frameworks and methodologies used to measure the UX in Smart Manufacturing, Section 5 provides challenges and Section 6 concludes this paper and outlines future work.

## II. OVERVIEW OF USER EXPERIENCE IN MANUFACTURING

During the mid-1700s, factories started to transition from hand production to implementing the use of machinery to help speed up their processes [5]. This started with the use of steam engines, that were modified by James Watt and Matthew Boulton to be powered by coal and water, however, they resulted in messy and polluted working conditions [6]. Nonetheless, it was agreed by economic historians that this era, the First Industrial Revolution (known today as Industry 1.0), was "the most important event in the history of humanity" [5]. It was developed by humans, to be used by humans, and the factory became the centre of community life [5].

Fast forward ~90 years to 1870, and the Industry 1.0 community was greeted with the technological power known as electricity. This Second Industrial Revolution era shaped the modern world we know today. By integrating electrification into their factories, manufacturers were able to speed up their production lines, which led to greater outputs. This meant society could go further in the world with the development of cars and aeroplanes [5]. This point in time, known today as Industry 2.0, had a positive impact on the world, as it transformed the lives of humans and gave them a purpose in life; what was once a factory built around a community became a connected society worldwide.

For the next 100 years, the manufacturing world continued to blossom, with the development of analogue technologies, to the integration of digital and partial automation [5]. This meant that the need for human assistance and intervention was starting to fade as advancements in computing technologies meant sectors, such as aerospace were able to make aeroplanes land themselves and robots could assemble products on the manufacturing production line, instead of people. This era, known as the Third Industrial Revolution (Industry 3.0), also had an impact on the level of education required to understand such systems. Thus what started as a simplistic UX that was accessible to all workers during the First Industrial Revolution became complex by the third. In essence, this made the factory that was once known as 'the centre of community life' inaccessible to the working class. Subsequently, the global supply chain volume increased and with it came economic change [5]. The once connected society of the world, became a fast global financial contest.

As the level of automation increased, more machines were able to communicate with one another more efficiently via networks, naming them as "cyber-physical production systems" [5]. From this, digitalisation was born and with it these machines were able to produce vast amounts of data. In order to extract additional data from these machines, IoT devices were integrated, which allowed for real-time data to be visualised on dashboards and for intelligent decisions to be made by incorporating the use of AI and Machine Learning (ML) algorithms. For example, monitoring the health and condition of machinery to predict and alert an engineer to fix the issue before it becomes a problem, potentially halting production [5]. In turn, this allowed manufacturers to be flexible in terms of their production, and "produce high-quality personalised products at mass efficiency" [7]. In 2011, this was introduced to the world as the Fourth Industrial Revolution (Industry 4.0) [7]. However, it is only within the last few years that companies are beginning to see the value that IoT devices can offer. This era is changing the way humans work, meaning it is more about the machine (drive productivity) than it is about the human using it.

As previously highlighted, the UX of each Industrial Revolution has become less focused on the human operating the machinery, and more on the production process and technology, as that is bringing in financial gains. Therefore, the relationship between human and machine has faded. However, with the advancements in digital technologies accelerating each year, the gap between each Industrial Revolution is becoming shorter.

In 2020, the Fifth Industrial Revolution was born (Industry 5.0) [7]. This version is setting out to assist in the personalisation and humanisation of digital technologies by putting the human back "at the centre of the production process" [7]. This means that the relationship that human and machine once had is now to be reconciled, by removing the barriers to create a meaningful experience for all users, and create a long-term service for humanity. Afterall, these technologies are designed to have a human component to interact with the system efficiently and effectively [8]. However, it was reported that 50% of supply chain leaders said merging technologies with existing talent is a challenge [3]. Therefore, for Industry 5.0, the UX of manufacturing applications must be flexible and adaptable to their users' needs, well-being, and intelligence. For example, cars made by Tesla learn how the driver interacts with the vehicle through their behaviours, usages, and devices, and adapts content to their needs in real-time [9]. However, some supply chain leaders have expressed concern relating to ethics and governance, and the supplying of correct information to a human worker based upon their level of access with the role they have been assigned to [3]. Nonetheless, Industry 5.0 now has the opportunity to bring a new workforce together (human and machine), and for them to become a decision-support as opposed to a decision-making mechanism in the production process [3].

## III. BACKGROUND TO INTERNET OF THINGS DEVICES

IoT devices play a vital role in the collection of additional data from machinery, assist with automating tasks, and enhance decision-making for humans. However, due to the gap between each industrial revolution getting shorter, these devices are still being rolled out today for some manufacturers. This is partly due to manufacturers being uneducated regarding the value these devices could bring to their business, and the cost for implementing such technology.

Since their initial launch in Industry 4.0, the price of IoT devices has come down and they are now affordable for most companies, especially those who utilise legacy machinery, as they can be a cost-effective alternative to purchasing new machines. By integrating these devices, they can enhance the overall production line by providing information on four key areas, such as products, people, processes, and infrastructure [10]. Devices consist of sensors, Radio-Frequency Identification (RFID) tags, and actuators to name a few [11]. These IoT devices are connected to a network that allows them to communicate with each other and provide a unified service to their user(s). When interacting with each other, this relationship is known as thing-to-thing, however, when a human interacts with an IoT device this relationship is referred to as human-thing [11].

With thing-to-thing, there are two subset levels of interaction, Internet and thing. Internet pertaining to the connection between other devices regarding quality and responsiveness to provide reliable services [11]. Whereas at thing level, this relates to its battery level (if applicable), energy consumption, interoperability, and installation difficulty to name a few [11]. Both levels impact the human-thing interaction, the UX behind it, the IoT system as a whole (interaction, privacy and security), and whether it is meeting the expectations and needs of its users [11].

The UX of IoT devices and their data is extended to the platforms they are connected to. The data collected from each device can be portrayed via a visual dashboard in a meaningful way for all members of the workforce to view, monitor, and assist with decision-making. One challenge with this is achieving interoperability – integrating outputs from a diverse range of devices produced by various manufacturers into a single platform, where they function together as one cohesive system. This enables data aggregation and analysis, providing valuable insights that support decision-making between humans and machines [3]. Platforms, such as Home Assistant are already accessible to members of the public to implement and experiment within the comfort of their own homes [12]. Systems like Home Assistant are necessary and relevant for the Smart Manufacturing realm to adopt and assist workers with their daily tasks. However, the UX surrounding these applications and how it can be enhanced to adapt and support not only its users, their intelligence and needs, but also current and future industrial revolutions is a question that remains.

## IV. Frameworks and Methodologies used to Measure the User Experience in Smart Manufacturing

The research indicates that when it comes to evaluating the UX of interfaces, they are predominantly associated with web applications and neglect industrial systems. It has been highlighted that there is a need for a tool, framework and/or methodology to assist with the evaluation and enhancement of Human Machine Interfaces (HMI) in industry, particularly within Industry 4.0 as it is associated with IoT devices [13].

Few emerging evaluation methods focus on the experience of IoT devices, though they are not necessarily within the realm of Smart Manufacturing. Nonetheless, they are of interest as they could be adaptable to other domains that incorporate such devices. For example, research conducted by Rodrigo et al. proposed a framework that consists of a checklist to conduct a UX evaluation of IoT scenarios [11]. This checklist was evaluated by Human Computer Interaction (HCI) experts and three versions were created to cater for a variety of users and their needs. For example, version one contained all the necessary fields, version two provided examples for those who are not as familiar with the checklist; and version three is a compact version offering visualisations.

The checklist consisted of measurements pertaining to the IoT scenarios ease of use (likert scale), applicability to all intended users, concreteness, clarity, ease of understanding, impartiality, parsimony, and pertinence to context [11]. To evaluate the checklist, users assessed the UX of a smart bulb to which positive results were obtained. This method highlighted that the checklist is suitable for evaluating the UX of IoT devices and assisting evaluators who may not be well-versed in the UX domain. Also, whilst this checklist was not tailored to the Smart Manufacturing domain, it has the potential to be used across a variety of realms. However, an area that it did lack was the assessment of an interface that an IoT device would portray its results to.

Research conducted by Aranburu et al. consisted of the creation of a tool known as eXperience Capturer (XC) [13]. It was developed due to the absence of evaluation tools specifically for the industrial HMI. The tool which is user-centred can be used in multiple ways, for example pre-interaction, during interaction, and post-interaction. It evaluates emotional and usability parameters during each phase mentioned, and combines quantitative and monitoring methods when a user conducts a test consisting of a series of tasks [13]. During testing it proved successful and emphasised the need for new methods to be utilised within the industrial domain to assist users with UX knowledge. By achieving this the communication and interaction between machine and user enhances and opens new avenues for technology to be implemented. However, whilst it was able to assist with the UX of HMI within an industrial domain, it lacked in the assessment of IoT devices where the interface is associated with and the human operator.

As highlighted throughout this paper, IoT devices provide additional information to users in the workplace and portray results via a visual interface. Whilst this is of interest, the relationship between human and machine (as well as thing) needs to improve.

Therefore, research conducted by Villani et al. proposes a general holistic framework known as INCLUSIVE [14]. This framework focuses on the connection between human and machine, as the researchers detail the "presence of human operators remains fundamental in industrial workplaces" [14]. Therefore, their work suggests the introduction of automation, whereby a machine adapts to the user's capabilities and effort and assists them with their working tasks [14]. This framework specifically targets Industry 4.0

and was tested within three domains: woodworking machinery for small companies, automation solutions in developing countries where operations are mostly manual and robotics are used during the assembly of appliances; and the management of large plants and warehouses with Laser-Guided Vehicles (LGV). This broad testbed showcases the frameworks flexibility and ability to relieve some complexity that modern production systems and operations bring to users by offering usable interfaces, with smooth and easy interaction [14].

The framework consists of three modules – measure, adapt, and teach [14]. Each module of the framework communicates together and use an adaptive automation middleware for hardware independence and modularity [14]. To understand their users more when moving around a machine, they utilised a wearable device known as Empatica E4 wristband, this captured their heart rate, skin temperature, and Galvanic skin response [14]. When they were not moving around a machine, their pupillary response was recorded via an eye tracking system. This research found that heart rate variability was one of the most responsive factors when measuring human reactions or strain. What is interesting, however, is that they found the higher levels of strain meant higher levels of satisfaction, as this was deemed as arousal and not stress, whilst good for short term, it could be harmful in long term [14]. Therefore, the amount of time between machine and human should be limited and breaks should be utilised.

Using each testbed, it was identified that the framework was accessible to all users irrespective of their age, education level, cognitive and physical impairments, and experience in the task to be performed. They also found that 80% of users became more productive and it helped them cooperate with machine/robot more efficiently [14]. By incorporating this framework, it allowed elderly, disabled or inexperienced users to stay in their jobs for longer, interact with complex automatic systems, and access working positions that they would be inaccessible to in other domains [14]. However, whilst this framework has proven to be successful with testbeds, there is still a lack of trust and acceptance from users. Therefore, before it could be implemented permanently, further research needs to be conducted (longitudinal tests) with users.

Research conducted by Johnston et al. presented a framework that is similar, meaning, it also measures three parameters, however, they are known as Dynamic, Adaptive, and Intelligent [15]. Dynamic refers to the contextual information surrounding the user, device, and their physical environment to provide a basic UX; Adaptive measures the user's capabilities and knowledge set to offer an enhanced UX; and Intelligent uses ML algorithms to deliver the appropriate interface by utilising user behavioural datasets [15]. This framework does not take into consideration the use of IoT devices. However, it could still be used in the manufacturing domain to assess the UX of IoT interfaces that portray data from sensors to workers from the workplace.

As previously outlined, manual work by humans is still a key area within the Smart Manufacturing domain, especially in terms of fixing defects in automated production lines. Research conducted by Stoll et al. proposes an Adaptive Visual Assistance systems using Spatial Augmented Reality (AVISAR) [16]. This framework adapts based on different repair tasks and the layout of a worker's manual assembly workstation, as well as the human themselves based on their skills and needs [16].

The user's assembly workstation is the key area of focus. The AVISAR framework utilises a projector to project information for the worker to utilise when working with an object. Information being projected consists of in-situ, where a faulty area of a circuit board is highlighted, and repair instructions which are displayed on the white surface [16]. This framework has the potential to work with IoT devices, for example, as future work the use of RFID tags could allow the system to recognise the user and adapt the workstation to suit their needs via saved user profiles, based on their level of education, disabilities, etc. [16]. By using a projector, it allows a user to utilise gestures, this indicates to the system that they are ready for the next stage of the repair task and for it to provide the next set of visual instructions. However, as this is a Spatial Augmented Reality (SAR) application, adaptations can be limited due to the type of projector and its projection rate. Therefore, the projector would have to be upgraded, and to allow for more scalable solution, the use of a Raspberry Pi would be implemented to make the deployment of the system more cost-effective and smaller (easier to use and implement) [16].

As highlighted, there are multiple solutions that can assist in the enhancement of IoT devices with the UX behind those and their associated interfaces. However, each company/organisation is unique, and one approach will not be suitable for all. Therefore, it is important for each organisation to "define and follow" a route that is both "structured and comprehensive", by achieving this it avoids "haphazardly" integrating new technologies in isolation [3].

## V. CHALLENGES

As highlighted throughout this paper there are several challenges, all of which remain unanswered. These challenges were derived through the identified gaps when conducting the scoping review and are defined below.

*1) Lack of a cohesive framework or methodology*

Firstly, there is not one framework or methodology that can cater to all the needs of industry, individuals, and IoT devices. As indicated from the research conducted, these have been identified as separate systems that focus on at least two of the three main parameters, but not as a collective.

By combining these three parameters, one framework would be established that could be used within Smart Manufacturing to assist with the enhancement of HMI and IoT technologies. By achieving this, the human-machine experience is enhanced whilst catering to the well-being of our workers and keeping the industry up to date with the latest Industrial Revolution.

*2) Lack of manufacturing focus when understanding the experience of IoT devices.*

As the implementation of Industry 5.0 draws closer (personalisation and humanisation), the requirement for systems to incorporate all three parameters is necessary, as it will require knowledge of the system, its user and the devices in which they are using as well as the task in hand. As portrayed, the use of IoT devices is still trickling its way through the manufacturing industry compared to others (Smart Home), and the UX underpinning these devices is still being evaluated by researchers.

In the realm of manufacturing, there have been setbacks when implementing such technologies, namely due to cost, lack of education, and not seeing its true potential. However, for this to change, the relationship between human, machine, and thing needs to improve. To achieve this, there needs to be trust and acceptance from all workers when machines attempt to adapt to their behaviours to offer a personal and humanised experience. As opposed to machines or technologies being implemented to replace workers, which typically brings negative experiences - this has been the most challenging area.

Therefore, by having a framework that is specifically for the manufacturing domain and the three parameters mentioned, this will in parallel, bring trust and acceptance to all workers, whilst enhancing the UX of IoT applications.

*3) Lack of a manufacturing interface for IoT devices.*

Today, there are ~18 billion connected IoT devices worldwide, with this figure set to almost double to 32.1 billion by 2030 [17], however, a challenge that remains in this area is interoperability. Some manufacturer's devices are 'locked' and only operate on their system; others are open-sourced and can be used with any interface. To overcome this, there should be a universal ethical approach to allow all IoT devices to be used with various systems, such as Home Assistant. It will be highly unlikely that one manufacturer will be able to produce all IoT devices for mankind. Therefore, at minimum, there should be one interface that can be used by all while understanding its user and the operational environment. Achieving this would, cater to the needs of Industry 5.0 and allows for most companies to transition to the next revolution with ease and less friction on training and financial costs. This would bring long term success and value to each company over time and the longevity of the products being made [3].

## VI. CONCLUSION AND FUTURE WORK

This paper has critically examined current frameworks and methodologies that have been created to enhance the human-machine experience of Smart Manufacturing systems, along with providing answers to the research questions previously defined.

In terms of limitations of the following review, there is a lack of research in the field of Smart Manufacturing on how to enhance the UX of IoT technologies. This is highlighted by the number of frameworks and methodologies identified and reviewed in this paper. This could also be due to the inclusion and exclusion criteria. Therefore, for future research, the amount of search terms would be increased. However, upon review, it was evident that this is an area that is starting to gain traction.

It has also been identified that most industrial companies are only now implementing IoT devices in their production due to costs coming down. However, the UX of these devices and their associated applications should focus on enhancing usability to better engage and support the user operating them. Therefore, each user's needs must be considered to adapt the interface appropriately, irrespective of their educational background and disabilities. Several frameworks are being developed; however, no such framework caters to Smart Manufacturing, the IoT device(s), and the system user. This is a remaining challenge and should be addressed in the future. By achieving this, it would allow manufacturers to reduce errors and become more resilient, whereby they are capable of minimising future uncertainties that may come down the tracks [18], whilst improving the human-machine relationship and the well-being of our workers.

As future work, Augmented Reality (AR) or Virtual Reality (VR) could be used to improve worker safety [19]. Training sessions with such technologies would allow the user to learn how they operate over time and highlight areas of concern and offer recommendations on how they could be addressed. The foundation of this method was highlighted via the use of a projector, however, this approach has the ability to adapt to the user, their needs and the task in hand. This method could incorporate the recommendation previously mentioned of having one interface and adapting to the IoT devices or machinery that is in its line of sight. In this way, the human-machine experience enhances and becomes one cohesive system whilst keeping the well-being of our workers a top priority. This recommendation acts as the scientific contribution of this paper and for Industry 5.0.

ACKNOWLEDGMENT

This research is funded by Innovate UK under the Smart Manufacturing Data Hub project (contract no. 10017032) – www.smdh.uk.

## REFERENCES

[1] S. Group, 'Industry 5.0 Designing User Experience for Smarter Manufacturing', Stefanini. Retrieved: Jan. 2025. [Online]. Available: https://stefanini.com/en/insights/news/industry-5-0-designing-user-experience-for-smarter-manufacturing

[2] M. Cai and J. Luo, 'Influence of COVID-19 on Manufacturing Industry and Corresponding Countermeasures from Supply Chain Perspective', *J. Shanghai Jiaotong Univ. (Sci.)*, vol. 25, no. 4, pp. 409–416, Aug. 2020, doi: 10.1007/s12204-020-2206-z.

[3] Deloitte, '2024 MHI Annual Industry Report - The Collaborative Supply Chain'. Material Handling Industry, 2024.

[4] D. Norman and J. Nielsen, 'The Definition of User Experience (UX)', Nielsen Norman Group. Retrieved: Jan. 2025. [Online]. Available: https://www.nngroup.com/articles/definition-user-experience/

[5] P. P. Groumpos, 'A Critical Historical and Scientific Overview of all Industrial Revolutions', *IFAC-*

*PapersOnLine*, vol. 54, no. 13, pp. 464–471, Jan. 2021, doi: 10.1016/j.ifacol.2021.10.492.

[6] BBC, 'When was the industrial revolution?', BBC Bitesize. Retrieved: Jan. 2025. [Online]. Available: https://www.bbc.co.uk/bitesize/articles/z6kg3j6

[7] X. Xu, Y. Lu, B. Vogel-Heuser, and L. Wang, 'Industry 4.0 and Industry 5.0—Inception, conception and perception', *Journal of Manufacturing Systems*, vol. 61, pp. 530–535, Oct. 2021, doi: 10.1016/j.jmsy.2021.10.006.

[8] M. Ardolino *et al.*, 'The impacts of digital technologies on coping with the COVID-19 pandemic in the manufacturing industry: a systematic literature review', *International Journal of Production Research*, vol. 62, no. 5, pp. 1953–1976, Mar. 2024, doi: 10.1080/00207543.2022.2127960.

[9] N. Ismail, 'Why IoT has failed to take off and the impact for the world when it does', Information Age. Retrieved: Jan. 2025. [Online]. Available: https://www.information-age.com/why-iot-has-failed-to-take-off-and-the-impact-for-the-world-when-it-does-17355/

[10] N. Santhosh, M. Srinivsan, and K. Ragupathy, 'Internet of Things (IoT) in smart manufacturing', *IOP Conf. Ser.: Mater. Sci. Eng.*, vol. 764, no. 1, p. 012025, Feb. 2020, doi: 10.1088/1757-899X/764/1/012025.

[11] R. L. A. Almeida, R. M. C. Andrade, T. G. R. Darin, and J. O. V. Paiva, 'CHASE: checklist to assess user experience in IoT environments', in *Proceedings of the ACM/IEEE 42nd International Conference on Software Engineering: New Ideas and Emerging Results*, in ICSE-NIER '20. New York, NY, USA: Association for Computing Machinery, Sep. 2020, pp. 41–44. doi: 10.1145/3377816.3381737.

[12] T. Rhujittawiwat *et al.*, 'Making smart platforms smarter: adding third party applications to home automation platforms', *J. Comput. Sci. Coll.*, vol. 37, no. 5, pp. 43–53, Oct. 2021.

[13] E. Aranburu, G. Lasa, J. K. Gerrikagoitia, and M. Mazmela, 'Case Study of the Experience Capturer Evaluation Tool in the Design Process of an Industrial HMI', *Sustainability*, vol. 12, no. 15, Art. no. 15, Jan. 2020, doi: 10.3390/su12156228.

[14] V. Villani *et al.*, 'The INCLUSIVE System: A General Framework for Adaptive Industrial Automation', *IEEE Transactions on Automation Science and Engineering*, vol. 18, no. 4, pp. 1969–1982, Oct. 2021, doi: 10.1109/TASE.2020.3027876.

[15] V. Johnston, M. Black, J. Wallace, M. Mulvenna, and R. Bond, 'A Framework for the Development of a Dynamic Adaptive Intelligent User Interface to Enhance the User Experience', in *Proceedings of the 31st European Conference on Cognitive Ergonomics*, in ECCE '19. New York, NY, USA: Association for Computing Machinery, Sep. 2019, pp. 32–35. doi: 10.1145/3335082.3335125.

[16] E. Stoll, J. Reiher, K. J. Gavali, and D. Kammer, 'AVISAR -- Adaptive Visual Assistance System using Spatial Augmented Reality for Manual Workplaces in Smart Factories', in *CEUR Workshop Proceedings*, Arenzano (Genoa), Italy: CEUR, Jun. 2024. Retrieved: Jan. 2025. [Online]. Available: https://ceur-ws.org/Vol-3704/paper11.pdf

[17] L. S. Vailshery, 'IoT connections worldwide 2022-2033', Statista. Retrieved: Jan. 2025. [Online]. Available: https://www.statista.com/statistics/1183457/iot-connected-devices-worldwide/

[18] K. Kapoor, A. Z. Bigdeli, Y. K. Dwivedi, and R. Raman, 'How is COVID-19 altering the manufacturing landscape? A literature review of imminent challenges and management interventions', *Ann Oper Res*, vol. 335, no. 3, pp. 1567–1599, Apr. 2024, doi: 10.1007/s10479-021-04397-2.

[19] D. Putri, I. Sriwana, and M. F. Safitra, 'Enhancing Workplace Safety Through Collaborative Technologies: A Case Study in the Manufacturing Industry', 2024, pp. 37–46. doi: 10.1007/978-981-99-8111-3_4.

# TrustLab$^{\text{TM}}$: An Interactive Tool for Evaluating Online Trustworthiness across Diverse Domains

Teng-Chieh Huang, Wenting Song, Brian Kim, and K. Suzanne Barber
*The University of Texas at Austin*
*The Center for Identity*
Austin, Texas, USA
e-mail: tengchieh@utexas.edu, wentingsong@utexas.edu, bkim994@utexas.edu, and sbarber@identity.utexas.edu

***Abstract*—TrustLab$^{\text{TM}}$ is an innovative online tool for assessing social media users' trustworthiness with ease and precision. It serves diverse users, from general social media participants to researchers aiming to gauge trust levels in various domains. Unlike many tools, TrustLab$^{\text{TM}}$ focuses on user trustworthiness rather than post content, distinguishing between experts and typical users. Using Trust Filters and user attributes, it assigns trust scores visualized through intuitive charts for clarity. Additionally, TrustLab$^{\text{TM}}$ provides personalized recommendations to help users enhance their online credibility. While its algorithms are domain-independent, this paper demonstrates TrustLab$^{\text{TM}}$'s application in finance, politics, and health, showcasing its role in shaping public discourse, knowledge, and connections. With its user-friendly interface, TrustLab$^{\text{TM}}$ is a significant tool for exploring and understanding online trust in the digital era.**

***Index Terms*—online trustworthiness; individual trust; social media; Trust Filter.**

## I. Introduction

Social media has transformed global communication, enabling rapid information sharing and connection. Platforms like X (formerly Twitter, 2006) popularized microblogging, while LinkedIn (2003) fostered professional networking, and Instagram (2010) and Snapchat (2011) emphasized visual sharing. Recently, TikTok (2016) has gained popularity for its short-form videos.

Alongside these benefits, social media has amplified the spread of misinformation, which can significantly impact public opinion on health, politics, and social issues. Misinformation on health topics, for instance, may discourage proper medical actions, while disinformation campaigns can manipulate public perception, influence elections, and create social discord. The rise of generative artificial intelligence (GenAI) further complicates trust by enabling realistic but misleading content, such as deepfake videos [1], [2].

To counter misinformation, platforms like X have implemented tools such as content flagging and partnerships with fact-checkers. Researchers also focus on approaches like rumor detection [3], [4] and bot detection [5]–[8]. This study introduces TrustLab$^{\text{TM}}$, a tool that uses six Trust Filters—authority, experience, expertise, identity, proximity, and reputation—to score user trustworthiness and rank users accordingly. TrustLab$^{\text{TM}}$ uses social media activity and user profiles to enhance trust in online discourse.

The contributions of this study are:

- Development of TrustLab$^{\text{TM}}$, an interactive tool scoring user trustworthiness.
- Application of TrustLab$^{\text{TM}}$ Trust Filters across finance, politics, and health domains.
- Comparison of TrustLab$^{\text{TM}}$ with other trust-evaluation tools, highlighting technology and method distinctions.

The remainder of this paper details the capabilities and algorithms of TrustLab$^{\text{TM}}$ (Section II), compares it with related works (Section III), and discusses future directions (Section IV).

## II. Exploring TrustLab$^{\text{TM}}$: Capabilities, Techniques, and Competitive Landscape

TrustLab$^{\text{TM}}$ applies machine learning to score social media posts using Trust Filters based on attributes like average post length, follower count, and post frequency. For instance, in finance and politics, a random forest regressor combined with these attributes showed high accuracy in assessing post trustworthiness [9]. We also found that different attributes are critical across domains: for example, restrained language is key in finance, while post frequency and experience are pivotal in health [10], [11].

Sentiment analysis, particularly on posts with emoticons, has proven effective for identifying trustworthy users, achieving over 80% accuracy [12]. The TrustLab$^{\text{TM}}$ Sentiment Trust Filter, for instance, has helped investors improve returns by following trustworthy sources. In health, Trust Filters were used to detect and forecast disease outbreaks, with epidemiologists tracing posts to monitor potential disease spread [13].

TrustLab$^{\text{TM}}$ has demonstrated positive results across diverse domains, such as finance, politics, and health [9]–[11]. This study focuses on these three areas where misinformation often affects user decision-making, underscoring the importance of high-quality information for better choices.

### A. *TrustLab$^{\text{TM}}$ Trust Filters: Scoring the Trust*

TrustLab$^{\text{TM}}$ scores user trustworthiness through filters like Experience, Reputation, Expertise, Authority, Identity, and Proximity. Each filter assigns scores (0-1) based on specific criteria, such as a user's social links, proximity to an event, or expertise level [11]. Additional attributes, like post length and punctuation use, further refine trust scores [9], [10]. TrustLab™ has shown high predictive accuracy (exceeding 99.99%) in identifying finance experts and users in financial discussions [10]. The algorithm also achieved accurate predictions in political events, such as the 2016 and 2020 U.S. elections, providing near-instant results at low computational cost.

### B. Target Domains Selection

To showcase TrustLab™'s versatility, we selected finance, health, and politics. These domains are highly influential, have substantial online misinformation, and can benefit from improved information quality. In finance, understanding public sentiment around stock market trends can help anticipate market movements. For politics, social media analysis has provided cost-effective and timely election forecasts [14]. In health, TrustLab™ has been used to monitor disease spread through trusted social media posts, enabling early response in biosurveillance applications like the Defense Threat Reduction Agency (DTRA) Biosurveillance Ecosystem (BSVE) [11].

By focusing on these areas, we demonstrate TrustLab™ as a robust tool for identifying trusted online information sources across varied domains. The following sections outline TrustLab™'s capabilities and potential use cases.

### C. Topic Selection and Trust Attributes Distribution

In the "Topics" section of TrustLab™ shown in Figure 1, we present comprehensive trust scores for each user, categorized by specific topics such as elections, the stock market, or various diseases. This section is broken down as follows: The "TrustLab™ Trust Filters" table (Table in Figure 1) ranks users by any targeted trust attribute or by the average score across all trust attributes, offering a nuanced view of user trustworthiness within specific contexts.

The "Trust Score Linear Distribution" chart (Figure 2a) illustrates the distribution of users across each trust attribute, with scores ranging from 0 to 1. This visual representation allows us to swiftly grasp the range and diversity of trustworthiness across different topics, thereby highlighting the spectrum of user credibility.

Furthermore, the "Trust Filter Score Per Source" chart (Figure 2b) details the composition of trust scores for the most or least trusted users. This facilitates an easy examination of the traits that distinguish highly trusted users from those deemed less reliable, thereby offering insights into the factors that contribute to a user's perceived trustworthiness.

Lastly, the "Source Network" chart (Figure 2c) maps out the social media connections among users based on their interactions, such as retweets, replies, or likes.

This chart effectively reveals clusters of social interconnections, thereby identifying the influencers within the network. Together, these visual tools provide a robust framework for analyzing and understanding the dynamics of trust across various topics on social media.

This section is designed to offer users the flexibility to explore a wide range of combinations pertaining to target domains, trust attributes, levels of trust, and intricacies of social network interconnections. For instance, researchers interested in delving deeper into the subject could use the distribution of trust attributes as a starting point to identify potentially significant attributes. Following this, TrustLab™ users can examine these specific trust attributes in more detail within the table, comparing them across different target domains to gain insight into their relative importance and application in various contexts.

In addition, we provide access to the original, unprocessed data for users who wish to conduct a thorough analysis of the results. This feature is especially valuable for those looking to explore raw data for more nuanced insights or to apply their own methodologies for data analysis.

In subsequent sections, we introduce other tools that offer refined results, thereby enabling users to efficiently leverage the TrustLab™ platform for a variety of purposes. These tools are designed to simplify the process of analyzing trust within social networks, making it more accessible to users to apply the platform's insights to their research or practical applications.

### D. Sources, Users, and Trustworthiness Assessment

*1) Comparison:* The "Comparison" tab in the TrustLab™ interface enables users to evaluate the trustworthiness of various topics and information sources, helping them make informed decisions about online information.

Users start by selecting a topic and a source (e.g., "Flu" and "CDC MMWR Quick Stats") as shown in Figure 3. Additional sources, like "WHO - Disease News", "BIOFEEDS HealthMap", and "WHER Reports", can be added to the comparison. Sources appear as green dots on the graph, and users can hover over these dots to view details or remove them with a click.

TrustLab™ also allows automatic comparison with the five most and least trusted sources (see Figure 4). By selecting specific Trust Filters, such as "Experience", users can see how sources compare based on individual or combined trust scores, making it easy to identify more trustworthy sources at a glance.

*2) Recommendation:* The "Score" section offers a detailed visualization of the trust scores for each trust attribute related to a specific user within a chosen topic. This allows for a direct comparison of an individual's trust scores with those of typical users and experts, including the variance observed within each group (Figure 5). This comparative analysis is based on the trust attribute extraction and group classification methodologies outlined by Huang et al. [9], [10].

Recommendations for enhancing a user's trustworthiness were derived from the findings of Huang et al. [9]. This research investigates strategies through which typical social media users might adjust their behaviors to bolster their trustworthiness and achieve recognition as experts in specific topics. To tailor these recommendations, a basin-hopping optimization algorithm was introduced by Wales et al. [15], is employed. This algorithm, known for its efficacy in global optimization, especially in complex, high-dimensional landscapes, applies

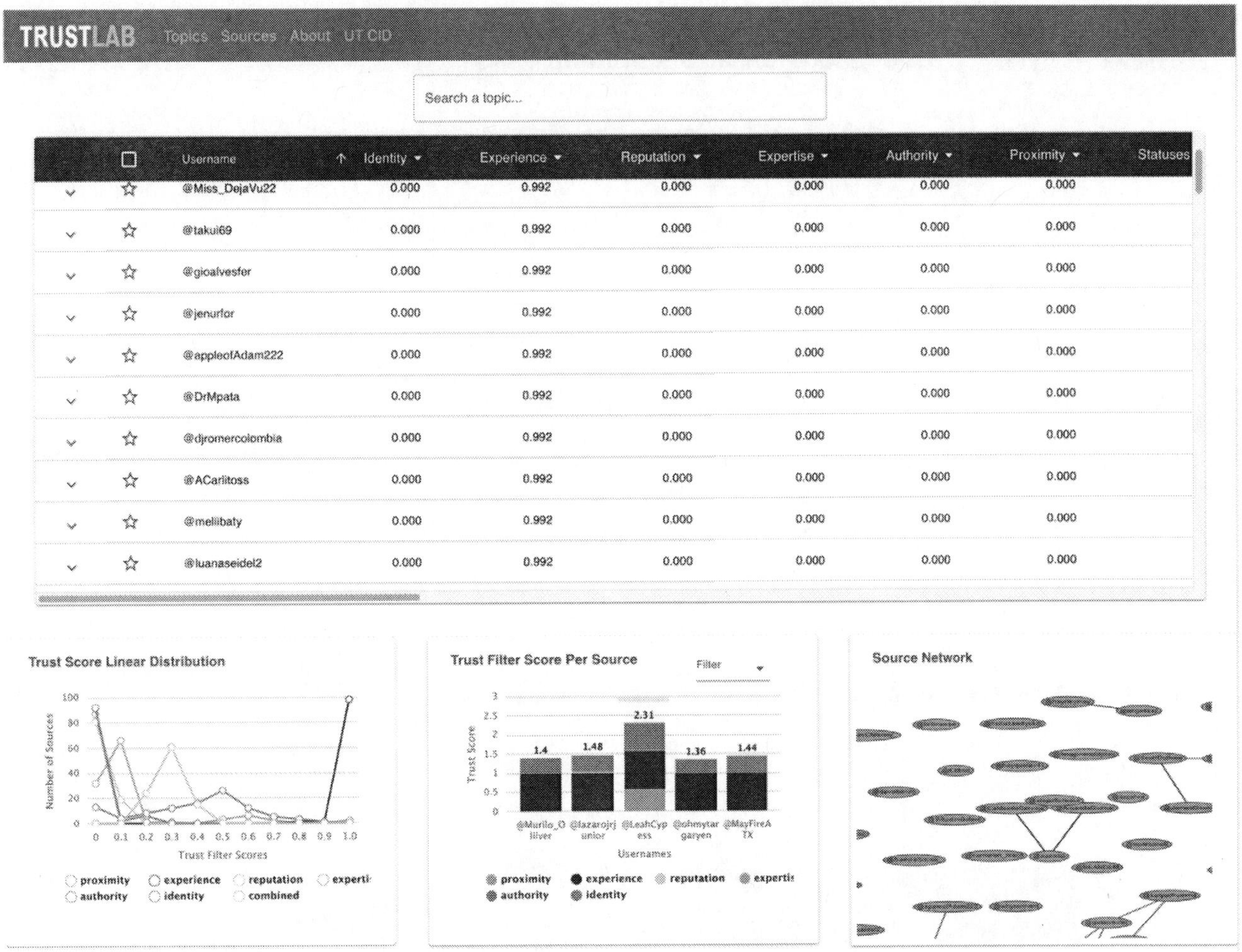


Fig. 1: Overview of Topics Page.

random perturbations to transcend local minima and employs a local search algorithm to refine solutions within each basin.

By comparing a specific user's trust scores with those of a typical user group and experts, the platform facilitates clear understanding of the disparities between them. Consequently, tailored trust score recommendations offer actionable guidance for users aiming to enhance their perceived trustworthiness on social media. This feature not only aids in personal or professional development but also contributes to the broader goal of fostering a more trustworthy and reliable digital community.

### E. Use Cases

In this section, the TrustLab™ use cases provided in Table I demonstrate potential application scenarios and utility for online users.

## III. TrustLab™ and a Comparison to Related Work

With the rise of social media as a primary source of news and information for many people, there is growing concern about the accuracy and reliability of the content shared on these platforms. Information trustworthiness on social media platforms is a critical issue that has attracted considerable research effort. Many systems and tools have also been developed to detect and counter misinformation, disinformation, or rumors.

Some studies have analyzed the content shared to assess its accuracy, bias, and potential for misinformation or disinformation. Using our tool, we assessed the trustworthiness of individuals sharing information. In this section, TrustLab™ is compared with seven state-of-the-art trust-related social media tools.

In Table II, TrustLab™ is compared with seven state-of-the-art trust-related tools highlighting the differences between these tools and discussing the pros and cons of each tool's technology, capabilities, and methods.

In Table III, several comparison metrics were selected to compare the representative tool features and functionality of these trust-related tools. First, we discuss the domains in which these tools have proven to be effective. Finance,

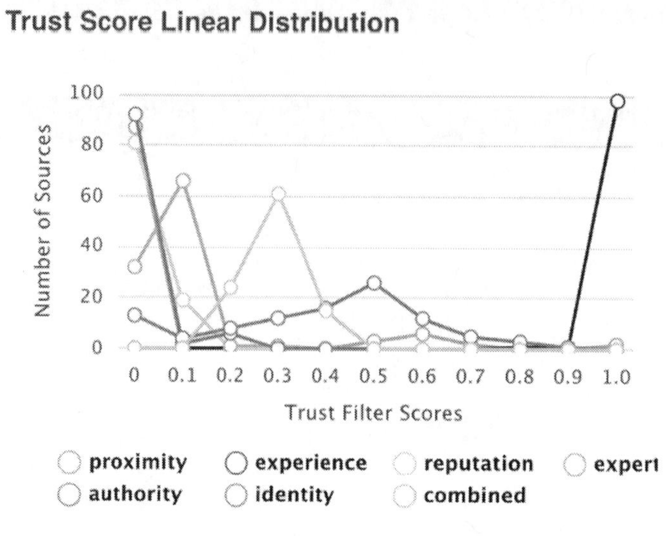


(a) Linear Distribution of the Trust Score.

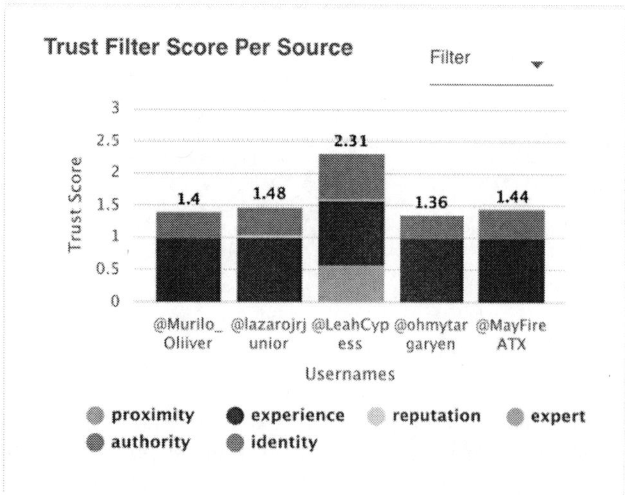


(b) Trust Score Per Source Graph.

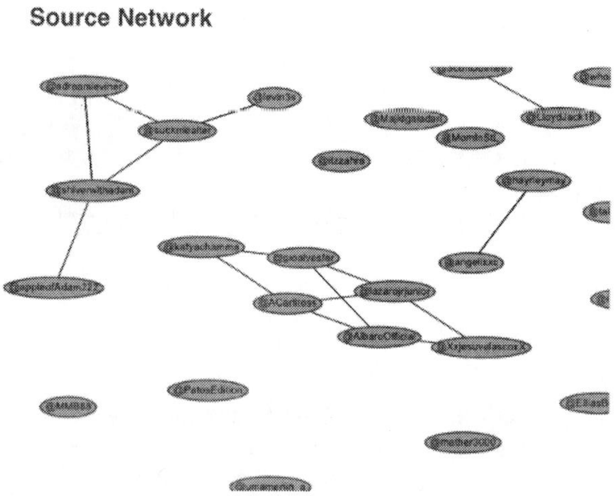


(c) Source Network Graph.

Fig. 2: Topics Page (Figure 1) Breakdown.

politics, and health are three of the most important domains, in which combating misinformation and disinformation is crucial. Some tools only perform experiments in a single domain or specific dataset, which limits their proven efficacy. Second, we compared the ability of the tool to differentiate between different objects. We evaluate the tool's ability to distinguish trusted information sources from malicious sources, trusted content from unreliable content, trusted users from untrusted users, or even bots. Third, we evaluate whether it is a platform-oriented tool or a user-oriented tool; in other words, whether it was developed to serve social media platforms such as X or whether it was developed to serve online users.

The comparison table highlights the distinct advantages of TrustLab$^{TM}$ over other existing solutions in the field. TrustLab$^{TM}$ excels for several reasons.

TrustLab$^{TM}$ goes beyond focusing on a single target domain in social media to encompass multiple domains. This versatility allows it to be applied across diverse areas related to public opinion or sentiment, thereby providing a comprehensive solution for trust assessment in various contexts.

It also demonstrates exceptional capabilities in differentiating users, content, and sources based on their trustworthiness. This granular approach enables the nuanced evaluation of trust dynamics within online communities, thereby enhancing the reliability of trust assessments.

TrustLab$^{TM}$ offers significant benefits to both users and

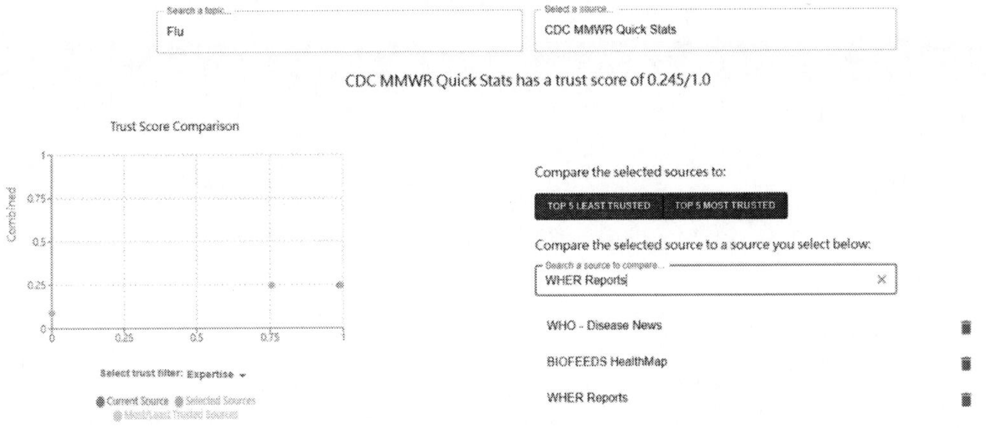


Fig. 3: Comparison Tab Sources Selection.

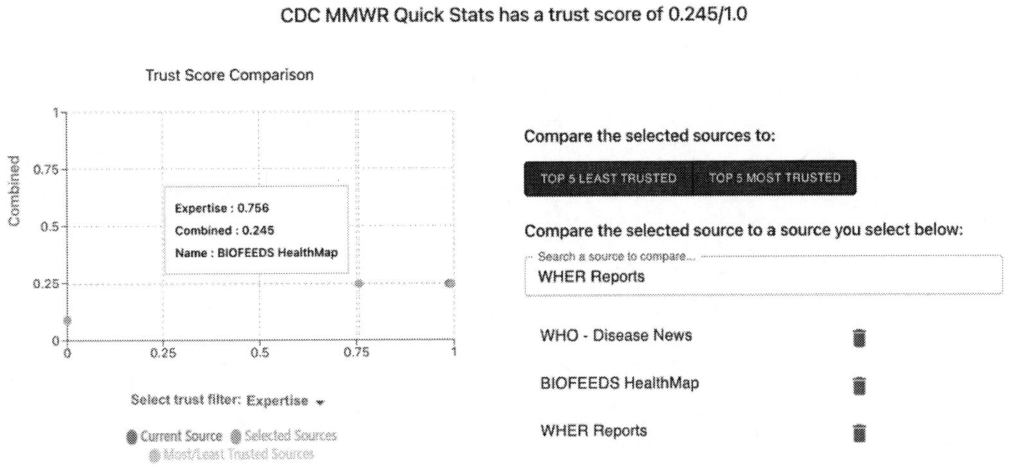


Fig. 4: Comparison Tab Source Info.

platforms. Addressing the needs of both stakeholders fosters a more trustworthy and transparent online environment, promoting positive interactions and informed decision-making.

In conclusion, TrustLab$^{TM}$'s multifaceted approach, combined with its user-centric design and platform integration, positions it as a leading tool for trust assessment in social media across various domains.

## IV. Conclusion and Future works

TrustLab$^{TM}$ is an effective tool for evaluating online trustworthiness, significantly enhancing the accuracy and reliability of digital interactions across various domains such as finance, politics, and health. By providing a clear metric to distinguish between credible and less trustworthy sources, TrustLab$^{TM}$ empowers users to make informed assessments of the information and information sources on which they rely to make decisions, fostering a safer and more transparent online environment. Moreover, the inclusion of personalized recommendations to improve individual trustworthiness is a standout feature of TrustLab$^{TM}$. These recommendations not only guide users in enhancing their own online presence but also contribute to the overall trustworthiness of digital communities by elevating the quality of interactions and information exchange. This dual capability of assessing and improving trust makes TrustLab$^{TM}$ a vital tool in the pursuit of more reliable and ethical online engagements.

Looking forward, the development roadmap for TrustLab$^{TM}$ includes several promising enhancements:

1) Customization of Trust Attributes: Enabling users to define or adjust trust attributes allows TrustLab$^{TM}$ to meet specific contextual needs, making it versatile across different platforms and user requirements.
2) Enhanced Integration and Accessibility: By improving integration with other tools and refining the user interface, TrustLab$^{TM}$ aims to become more accessible to a broader audience, including those with limited technical expertise, thus expanding its utility and effectiveness.

These initiatives aim to further cement TrustLab$^{TM}$'s role as a cornerstone technology for enhancing the integrity and relia-

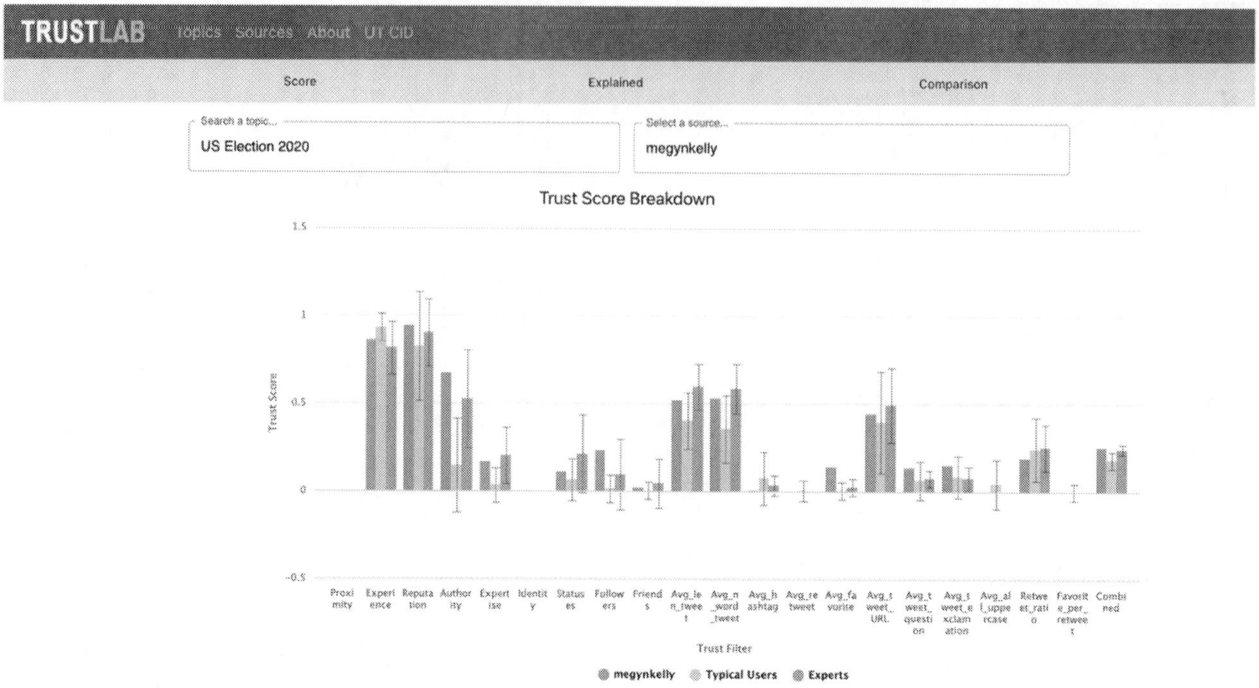


Fig. 5: Trust Score Breakdown.

TABLE I: USE CASES OF TrustLab™ TRUST FILTERS.

| **Use Scenarios** | **Application Notes** |
|---|---|
| To study online trust indicators | The Trust Score Table (Figure 1) shows calculated trust scores of X users on seven trust attributes: Authority, Experience, Expertise, Identity, Proximity, and Reputation. |
| To analyze trust score distribution for a topic | The Trust Score Linear Distribution Chart (Figure 1) displays trust score distribution for a topic. Low trust among most sources may indicate misinformation requiring further research. |
| To examine relationships between information sources | The Source Network Graph (Figure 1) represents sources as nodes and shows their connections, illustrating proximity and relevance. |
| To evaluate trustworthiness across topics and sources | The Trust Score Comparison Scatter Plot (Figure 4) identifies the top five most and least trustworthy sources. The Linear Distribution Chart also highlights overall trust levels for each topic. |
| To identify high- and low-quality sources on social media | The Trust Score Per Source Graph (Figure 1) presents stacked trust scores for each attribute, identifying the most and least trustworthy sources. |
| To obtain a source's trust score on specific attributes | The Trust Score Explained page (Figure 6) details trust scores by attribute, helping users make informed decisions. |
| To understand how trust is built online | The About pages (Figure 7) explain the computation of the seven trust attributes, giving an overview of how trustworthiness is measured. |
| To receive advice on improving trust scores and influence | The Trust Score Breakdown page (Figure 5) offers suggestions for increasing social media credibility and reach within specific fields. |

TABLE II: TECHNICAL COMPARISON WITH TRUST-RELATED TOOL COUNTERPARTS FOR SOCIAL MEDIA.

| **Trust Tools for social media** | **Technology** | **Capabilities** | **Methods** |
|---|---|---|---|
| TrustLab$^{TM}$ Trust Filters | Random Forest Classification; Random Forest for Time Series Prediction; Basin Hopping Optimization | A tool to find trusted information on social media by filtering and scoring trusted users. Ability to classify user groups based on trustworthiness and provide recommendations on improving trustworthiness for users. | Quantify user trustworthiness under multiple trust attributes, and performs expert detection and trustworthy user ranking. |
| Bot Sentinel [16] | Machine Learning Classification | A platform that classifies and tracks inauthentic accounts and toxic trolls on X. Records marked accounts in a database. | Classify and scores accounts based on how likely the account engages in nefarious activities, which may result in the spread of disinformation. |
| Mendoza et al. [5] | PyTorchBigGraph (PBG); Proximity Graph; In-order Traversal | A semi-supervised algorithm to distinguish between bots and legitimate users. This work also examined the impact of malicious accounts on the spread of misinformation. | Demonstrate the existence of different robot clusters through label propagation and interaction graph analysis. Identified potential areas where misinformation could have spread. |
| Lukasik et al. [17] | Gaussian Process; Multi-task Learning; Natural Language Processing (NLP) | A transfer learning approach for classifying stances in tweets discussing emerging rumors. | Determine aggregate stance of a rumor, which has been shown to generally correlate with actual rumor veracity. Enables users to be more informed on the validity of rumors on X. |
| Gilani et al. [6] | Behavioral Analysis; Interaction Graphs | A comparative analysis of bots and legitimate users on Twitter (X). This work uncovers differences in account behavioral characteristics between bots and humans to facilitate bot detection. | Reveal the profound impact on the spread of information upon removing bots from X. Although bots are a major factor in the spread of misinformation and rumors, the detriment on the overall spread of any information may outweigh the benefits of removing bots. |
| SENTINEL [18] | Machine Learning Classification; Deep Neural Networks | A software system to classify health-related tweets and detect disease outbreaks. It also provides instant predictions of current disease levels. | Combat misinformation in posts by validating them with information from other trustworthy news and data sources. Ensures users receive correct and verified information. |
| Nizzoli et al. [19] | User Similarity Network | A network-based framework for detecting coordinated behavior and discovering coordinated communities on social media. This work also characterizes the coordination patterns that emerge in different community behaviors. | Analyze the similarity and degree of coordination in posts. May give insight into potential organized misinformation or rumors. Unable to confidently determine if coordination was intentional or coincidental. |
| TrollPacifier [20] | Sentiment Analysis; ActoDeS Framework | A holistic system for troll detection of users on Twitter (X) with high accuracy. | Address potential disinformation by identifying accounts with potentially malicious behaviors. |

TABLE III: FUNCTIONAL COMPARISON WITH TRUST-RELATED TOOL COUNTERPARTS FOR SOCIAL MEDIA.

| **Trust Tools for Social Media** | **Target Domains** | | | | **Ability to Distinguish** | | | **Developed to Serve** | |
|---|---|---|---|---|---|---|---|---|---|
| | Finance | Politics | Health | Other | Sources | Content | Users | Platform | Users |
| TrustLab$^{TM}$ Trust Filters | ✔ | ✔ | ✔ | | ✔ | ✔ | ✔ | ✔ | ✔ |
| Bot Sentinel [16] | | | | | | ✔ | ✔ | ✔ | ✔ |
| Mendoza et al. [5] | | | | Music | | | ✔ | ✔ | |
| Lukasik et al. [17] | | | | N/A | | ✔ | ✔ | ✔ | |
| Gilani et al. [6] | | | | N/A | | | ✔ | ✔ | |
| SENTINEL [18] | | | ✔ | | ✔ | ✔ | | ✔ | ✔ |
| Nizzoli et al. [19] | | ✔ | | | | | ✔ | ✔ | |
| TrollPacifier [20] | | | | N/A | | ✔ | ✔ | | ✔ |

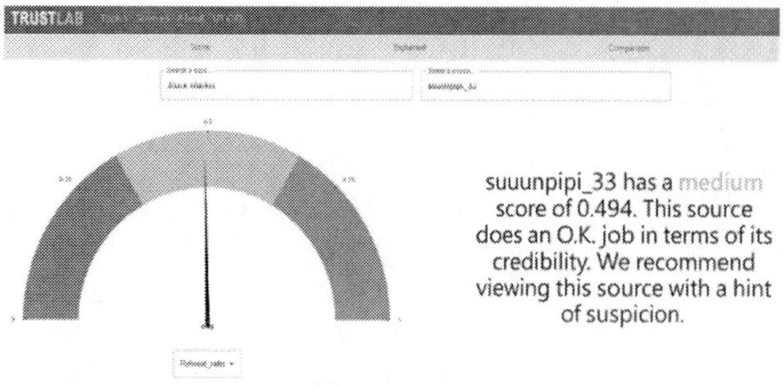


Fig. 6: Trust Score Explained.

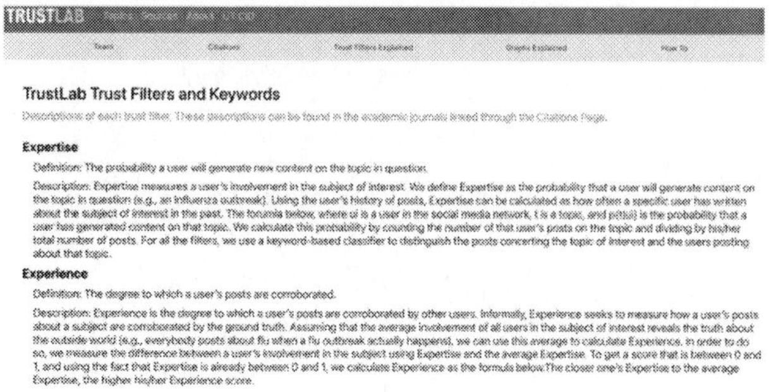


Fig. 7: TrustLab[TM] Trust Filters Explanation.

bility of online content, ensuring that it continues to contribute effectively to the trustworthiness of digital communication.

## References


[1] I. Goodfellow *et al.*, "Generative adversarial nets," *Advances in neural information processing systems*, vol. 27, 2014.

[2] D. P. Kingma and M. Welling, "Auto-encoding variational bayes," *arXiv preprint arXiv:1312.6114*, 2013.

[3] A. Zubiaga, A. Aker, K. Bontcheva, M. Liakata, and R. Procter, "Detection and resolution of rumours in social media: A survey," *Acm Computing Surveys (Csur)*, vol. 51, no. 2, pp. 1–36, 2018.

[4] C. Naumzik and S. Feuerriegel, "Detecting false rumors from retweet dynamics on social media," in *Proceedings of the ACM web conference 2022*, 2022, pp. 2798–2809.

[5] M. Mendoza, M. Tesconi, and S. Cresci, "Bots in social and interaction networks: detection and impact estimation," *ACM Transactions on Information Systems (TOIS)*, vol. 39, no. 1, pp. 1–32, 2020.

[6] Z. Gilani, R. Farahbakhsh, G. Tyson, and J. Crowcroft, "A large-scale behavioural analysis of bots and humans on twitter," *ACM Transactions on the Web (TWEB)*, vol. 13, no. 1, pp. 1–23, 2019.

[7] G. Lingam, R. R. Rout, D. V. Somayajulu, and S. K. Das, "Social botnet community detection: a novel approach based on behavioral similarity in twitter network using deep learning," in *Proceedings of the 15th ACM Asia Conference on Computer and Communications Security*, 2020, pp. 708–718.

[8] H. Peng *et al.*, "Unsupervised social bot detection via structural information theory," *arXiv preprint arXiv:2404.13595*, 2024.

[9] T.-C. Huang and K. S. Barber, "Using historical social media retrieved trust attributes to help distinguishing trustworthy users," *INTELLI 2023*, p. 21, 2023.

[10] T.-C. Huang, R. N. Zaeem, and K. S. Barber, "Identifying real-world credible experts in the financial domain," *Digital Threats: Research and Practice*, vol. 2, no. 2, pp. 1–14, 2021.

[11] R. N. Zaeem, D. Liau, and K. S. Barber, "Predicting disease outbreaks using social media: Finding trustworthy users," in *Proceedings of the Future Technologies Conference (FTC) 2018: Volume 1*. Springer, 2019, pp. 369–384.

[12] T.-C. Huang, R. N. Zaeem, and K. S. Barber, "It is an equal failing to trust everybody and to trust nobody: Stock price prediction using trust filters and enhanced user sentiment on twitter," *ACM Transactions on Internet Technology (TOIT)*, vol. 19, no. 4, pp. 1–20, 2019.

[13] G. Lin, R. N. Zaeem, H. Sun, and K. S. Barber, "Trust filter for disease surveillance: Identity," in *2017 Intelligent Systems Conference (IntelliSys)*. IEEE, 2017, pp. 1059–1066.

[14] T.-C. Huang, R. N. Zaeem, and K. S. Barber, "Finding trustworthy users: Twitter sentiment towards us presidential candidates in 2016 and 2020," in *Intelligent Systems and Applications: Proceedings of the 2021 Intelligent Systems Conference (IntelliSys) Volume 2*. Springer, 2022, pp. 804–821.

[15] D. J. Wales and J. P. Doye, "Global optimization by basin-hopping and the lowest energy structures of lennard-jones clusters containing up to 110 atoms," *The Journal of Physical Chemistry A*, vol. 101, no. 28, pp. 5111–5116, 1997.

[16] C. Bouzy, "Bot sentinel," https://botsentinel.com/, [retrieved: Jan, 2025].

[17] M. Lukasik *et al.*, "Gaussian processes for rumour stance classification in social media," *ACM Transactions on Information Systems (TOIS)*, vol. 37, no. 2, pp. 1–24, 2019.

[18] O. Şerban, N. Thapen, B. Maginnis, C. Hankin, and V. Foot, "Real-time processing of social media with sentinel: A syndromic surveillance system incorporating deep learning for health classification," *Information Processing & Management*, vol. 56, no. 3, pp. 1166–1184, 2019.

[19] L. Nizzoli, S. Tardelli, M. Avvenuti, S. Cresci, and M. Tesconi, "Coordinated behavior on social media in 2019 uk general election," in *Proceedings of the International AAAI Conference on Web and Social Media*, vol. 15, 2021, pp. 443–454.

[20] P. Fornacciari, M. Mordonini, A. Poggi, L. Sani, and M. Tomaiuolo, "A holistic system for troll detection on twitter," *Computers in Human Behavior*, vol. 89, pp. 258–268, 2018.